THE TEMPLE IN THE GARDEN

PRIESTS AND KINGS

DINAH DYE
FOREWORD BY BODIE THOENE

The Temple Revealed in the Garden: Kings and Priests

By Dinah Dye

Foundations in Torah Publishing

Unless otherwise noted, Scripture quotations are taken from the
Tree of Life Version (TLV) Messianic Jewish Family Bible Society.
Copyright © 2015.

ISBN 978-0-9972410-2-0

Visit the author's website at www.FoundationsInTorah.com

IN HONOR OF

שלום בן הירשאל

Saul Brottman
1923 – 2016

May His Memory be for a Blessing!

WWII veteran
Husband of Harriette for 65 years
Father of Diane and Janice
Grandfather of Hannah, Sarah, and Kyle
Great-grandfather of Ya'el, Gavriella, Remy, and Hezekiah
And all the precious seed that will follow

CONTENTS

FOREWORD

We often say that "everything means something." Through deep study of the Hebrew roots of Torah, we find there is not one small detail in the ancient text that is not significant. In Matthew 5:17–18, *Yeshua* confirms this when He declares, "Do not think that I came to destroy the Law or the Prophets. I did not come to destroy but to fulfill. For assuredly, I say to you, till heaven and earth pass away, one jot or one tittle will by no means pass from the law till all is fulfilled."

It is also true that "we don't know what we don't know." Reading the truth in Scripture can make us feel a lot like a man who has lived in the desert his entire life. He climbs to a mountaintop and sees the ocean for the very first time. The sunlight reflects on the surface, and he cannot tell if he is looking at water or a solid sheet of silver. If it is water, is it two inches deep? Or is it of limitless depth, filled with wonders beyond his imagination? How can we know the depth of scriptural meaning and truth unless we stand beside it, touch it, and find the courage to plunge into it?

Dr. Dinah Dye's deeply anointed Biblical scholarship takes us on a spiritual journey of ultimate discovery. As I read the text, it was like diving into the clear, deep waters of the sea and being able to breathe! Oh, the wonders in these passages! I began to understand just how much glory there is to be revealed beneath the surface.

When *Yeshua* spoke to us and said that not even the smallest Hebrew letter would pass away, He was letting us know that in the depths of Torah study there is life and beauty and color and the glory of Paradise revealed! Torah is also like a great tree with branches set like rungs in a ladder. We may climb up and up until we finally enter in. Truth is there in Scripture for us — the significance of all things great and small.

This incredible book helps show us the wonders of God's great love and plan for us from the very beginning of creation. If you want to glimpse great and holy wonders, I highly recommend this beautiful book. It is for you who want to explore the unknown beauty beneath the surface of the deep waters of Torah. It is for you who long to climb the branches of the tree that reaches from earth, high into heaven's glories.

Enjoy the journey!
Shalom and blessings!
Bodie Thoene
www.Thoenebooks.com

ACKNOWLEDGMENTS

Sarah Hawkes Valente: chief among editors
David Farley: layout/designer
Robin Hanley: cover designer
Tyler Dawn Rosenquist: content editor
Margo Doll: proofreader
Hannah Romero: proofreader

The earth is *Adonai's* and all that fills it —
the world, and those dwelling in it.
For He founded it upon the seas,
And established it upon the rivers.
Who may ascend the mountain of *Adonai?*
Who may stand in His holy place?
One with clean hands and a pure heart,
Who has not lifted his soul in vain,
Nor sworn deceitfully.
He will receive a blessing from *Adonai,*
Righteousness from God his salvation.

(PSALM 24.1–5)

PROLOGUE

Adonai has set up His throne in the heavens,
And His kingdom rules over all.
(Psalm 103.19)

In the beginning, *Elohim* built a Temple called the Heavens and the Earth. Through Wisdom, Knowledge, and Understanding, the master craftsman formed His cosmic House from the dew of the seventh heaven, and He blew the breath of life into His creation. The *Ruach* (Spirit) of G-d hovered over the face of the waters like a mother bird building her nest.

Elohim cut a covenant, and His word bound Heaven and Earth together in marriage. Unity was sealed forever in the place where blazing tongues of fire radiate from the Throne of Glory — G-d's Holy Oracle. A sign in the heavens confirmed His eternal oath: water and fire fused to fashion a rainbow-colored arc that connected Heaven to Earth.

Elohim laid immense beams over the upper waters, and He stretched out His chamber from one end of Heaven to the other. Inside the folds of His garment, vaults were filled with Heaven's fresh waters. He carpeted His tent with thick darkness and hung a crystalline veil at its entrance. Cherubim clasping flaming swords stood like sentries at the opening of the firmament: a dome-shaped lid that covered the earth. *Elohim's* chariot throne rested on parti-colored sapphire paving stones where a river of fire burst forth from underneath His earthly footstool. The king was clothed in dazzling light; He was dressed in splendor and majesty.

Soaring above the horizon, *Elohim* rode His glorious chariot on the wings of a storm. He divided His lower chamber into seven *Yamim* (days or stages) to mirror the upper. *Elohim* separated feminine elements from masculine: Earth from Heaven, light from darkness, waters below from waters above, land from sea, night from day. After the seas gathered and dry land appeared, He fastened Earth's throne to a massive obsidian rock. Atop the foundation stone, He set a pure gold rectangular-shaped box filled with His seed, then He placed a golden lid upon it.

Elohim fashioned His lower House into three courtyards and filled each with His possessions: Heaven, the inner sanctum, contained all the celestial bodies. Earth, the inner courtyard, was filled with seed-producing plants, trees, and grasses. The seas formed the outer courtyard for the fish and great sea monsters that populated the deep. His lower house became the boundary that prevented the waters of chaos from crossing over.

On the seventh day, *Elohim* inaugurated His completed Temple for service. Creation rested; His royal house was filled with the fire of His glory. Accompanied by one hundred blasts of a ram's horn, the hosts of Heaven paid homage to the Creator of the universe with shouts of joy and acclamation. The heavenly chorus worshipped, singing, "All Praise and Honor, Glory and Majesty, Blessing and Triumph, Dominion and Power to the Sovereign King." *Elohim's* throne was firmly established in the heavens; His Kingdom reigned over all.

At the climax of His creation, *Elohim* installed the human, Adam, as king and high priest to rule over the garden in Eden — located at the center of the cosmos. Adam sprouted up from the dust of the earth to become a mighty tree. His shade would cover the earth's mountains. As king, he was to maintain order and stability — serving as the mediator between Heaven and Earth. As *Elohim's* divine image-bearer, Adam was called to spread G-d's seed and to expand the garden to Earth's four corners. He was to rule the world in righteousness, justice, and peace and to preserve the created order through acts of worship so chaos could not destroy the *Shalem* (peace).

Eden was *Elohim's* perfection where He dwelled "in the midst" of His creation. It was the Temple where His seed was sown to produce a harvest in His image and likeness. His seed was His most treasured possession!

CHAPTER ONE

EDEN

For Adonai will comfort Zion,
He will comfort all her waste places,
He will make her wilderness like Eden,
her desert like the garden of Adonai.
Joy and gladness will be found in her,
thanksgiving and a sound of melody.
(Isaiah 51.3)

From Architecture to Agriculture

The Psalmist's creation account describes the construction of a cosmic temple using architectural terms: laying the beams, stretching out the tent, erecting the curtains, sinking the pillars in the earth, setting the cornerstone (Ps. 104). John Lundquist describes the temple as the "architectural embodiment of the cosmic mountain" (1984: 57). Scholars refer to the mountain as the *axis mundi* or connecting point between Heaven and Earth. It was the source of cosmic order and the barrier against chaos. Mount Zion was seen as the entrance into the celestial world. Also, in the ANE (ancient Near East), Wisdom was the key architectural expression for temple building. This attribute, bestowed upon a king by his god, gave him the authority to rule rightly.

> By employing building terminology in the creation story, the priestly author has done nothing new, but has joined other biblical writers who describe the world as a building, the Creation as an act of building, and the Creator as a wise, knowledgeable and discerning architect.
>
> (HUROWITZ 1992: 242)

> By Wisdom is a house built, by understanding it is made secure, and by knowledge its rooms are filled with all kinds of costly and precious, pleasant possessions.
>
> (PROVERBS 24.3,4)

> G-d gave wisdom and discernment in great measure and a breath of understanding as vast as the seashore. Solomon's wisdom surpassed the wisdom of all the sons of the east and all the wisdom of Egypt.
>
> (I KINGS 5.9,10)

The work of creation was described as "very good," which meant it was fully functional. In Genesis (2,3), the language shifts from architectural to agricultural, that is, the sustenance and maintenance of creation. This change in focus required a different kind of work — now the responsibility of the human, Adam, who was placed in the garden. Adam (mankind) was to serve as a royal priesthood — a Kingdom of priests. NT Wright describes this work as a man's "covenant vocation." He suggests "the main task of the vocation is 'image-bearing,' reflecting the Creator's wise stewardship into the world and reflecting the praises of all creation back to its maker" (Wright 2016: 76).

The Odes of Solomon (38:17–21) describe the saint as one who is established on foundations that were laid, and, as a cultivation, watered by G-d. GK Beale explains, "[T]hese traditions build upon the fact that in the Old Testament, the Garden of Eden, Israel's garden-like promised land, and Israel's future restoration in a garden-like land were either equated or associated with a temple" (2004: 246). The Apostle Paul suggested something similar when he compared the Corinthian congregation to a field — an idiom that is related to the Temple.

> For we are G-d's co-workers; you are G-d's field, G-d's building. According to the grace of G-d who was given to me, like a skilled master builder, I laid a foundation, and another builds on it. But let each consider carefully how he builds on it. For no one can lay any other foundation than what is already laid — which is *Yeshua* the Messiah.
>
> (I CORINTHIANS 3.9–11)

Temple services and ceremonies performed by priests were synonymous with Adam cultivating a garden: plowing, sowing, reaping, fertilizing, pruning, and harvesting. The production of plant life was tied to the *eretz* (dry land) which allowed the creation process to continue. "An agrarian society was dependent on the cycles of nature, and so agricultural imagery was a frequently used metaphor to describe G-d's nature and His divine power to bring about abundance" (Meyers 2003: 135–137). In Jerusalem's Temple, eating was the highest form of worship; in the garden, food production was how the community survived. "This relationship between humans and the earth and their destiny to practice agriculture becomes important in the epic history of *Yahweh's* chosen people" (George and George 2014: 135).

In the ANE, priests worked the fields to provide food for the deity. The king, on the other hand, maintained order and stability through cultivation and built massive garden complexes to create an aesthetically beautiful environment for pure enjoyment. In Mesopotamia, horticulture was the vocation of kings, and thus these rulers were referred to as "gardeners." The sovereign's royal gardens represented his kingdom and were in many ways similar to the famed English country estates with their pools, water courses, and winding paths through tall shrubs and shade trees. The royal garden was a cosmic temple in miniature.

> Every king had his garden, and Jerusalem's King was no exception. On the west bank of the Kidron valley, east of the fortified city was the 'king's garden,' watered by the Gihon spring. The royal garden of Jerusalem, the city of G-d, was in some sense a replication of, or perhaps the basis for, the primordial garden of Eden in Genesis.
>
> (BROWN 2010: 91)

After conquering territories, a suzerain would abscond with the defeated king's royal shrubbery to replant in his gardens. "Assyrian annals indicate that kings were as proud of their horticultural expertise as they were of their prowess on the battlefield. They frequently transplanted the exotic botanical species of conquered territories, boasting that they thrived better under their green thumb than in their natural habitats" (Brown). The kingdom was their garden, and their ordained task was to cultivate it.

The First Temple, built by King Solomon, featured many garden elements (I Kings 6). He possessed knowledge of botany and spoke in depth of "trees, from the cedar in Lebanon to the hyssop that grew in the wall, and about beasts, birds, creeping things and fish" (4.33). King Solomon paneled the inside walls of the Temple and carved ornamental cedarwood buds, open flowers, cherubim, and palm trees into each panel. The floors were overlaid with planks of cypress. The olivewood doors to the inner sanctuary were also adorned with cherubim, palm trees, and flowers — all overlaid with fine gold. Solomon dedicated time and energy to building the impressive royal gardens.

> I increased my possessions. I built myself houses and I planted myself vineyards. I made royal gardens and parks for myself and planted all kinds of fruit trees in them. I constructed for myself pools of water to irrigate a forest of flourishing trees.
>
> (ECCLESIASTES 2.4–6)

Ancient texts describe lavish gardens built by the Sumerians, Assyrians, and Babylonians in the alluvial plains of southern Mesopotamia. No archaeological evidence has been found for the existence of King Nebuchadnezzar's Hanging Gardens of Babylon — even though it was considered one of the seven wonders of the ancient world. (ANE scholar Stephanie Mary Dalley has suggested the hanging gardens were built by King Sennacherib in the city of Nineveh). It is thought Nebuchadnezzar built the magnificent gardens for his consort who longed for mountainous environs. The rooftop gardens were said to resemble a large mountain formed by terraces and supported by sunbaked brick columns. Trees rooted in the soil-filled columns gave the garden its hanging appearance.

Persian gardens were designed along a central axis likened to the world pillar or world tree (known as the *axis mundi*) to create a cosmic symmetry. In Mari, the walls of the palace courtyard enclosed the garden which was called the Court of the Palms. The central feature of the gardens in Ugarit was the royal tree: a date palm or tamarisk. Palm trees were a popular motif on temple facades which, according to Dalley, "represented groves of trees, in touch with the underworld, surrounding a high mountain, in touch with the sky." Ancient temples featured stylized trees, columns, and pillars that facilitated access to the divine and represented the temple as a sacred center. "Sacred trees and their derivative form of the pillar/column had an 'architectural function' in cosmic geography, serving to hold up the heavens" (quoted George and George 2014: 141 from Philpot 1897: 128). Trees also enhanced the pride of the city and took a central position in temple and palace courtyards; their edible fruit recreated the garden paradise and signified the achievement of peace and harmony.

Hard work created a successful garden. In the land of Israel, fields and hillsides were cleared of stones — which were later fashioned into terraces and walls. Gardens built on mountainsides required large quantities of soil plus a regular supply of water. The plains of southern Mesopotamia were watered by the Tigris and Euphrates Rivers, whereas the great cities of Egypt were fed by the Nile; both benefited from irrigation canals. Jerusalem, however, located on a mountaintop, was without a river as a water source. Rainwater collection remained seasonal, and so a network of cisterns and reservoirs became essential for survival in the ancient capital. Life could not exist without water; a dry cistern meant certain death.

Water from the Gihon Spring supplied Jerusalem with its drinking water and irrigated the king's garden. Considered the "fountainhead" of the waters of creation that flowed out to the whole world, the Gihon was the location for the coronation of the rulers of Israel. Solomon rode King David's mule down to the Gihon where Zadok, the priest, and Nathan, the prophet, anointed him. "Blow the shofar and say: Long live King Solomon! He shall come and sit on my throne. For he shall be king in my place, as I have appointed him to be ruler over Israel and Judah" (I Kings 1.32–35). Walton explained,

> The garden adjoins G-d's residence in the same way that a garden of a palace adjoins the palace. Eden is the source of the waters and the residence of G-d. The text describes a situation that was well known in the ancient world: a sacred spot featuring a spring with an adjoining well-watered park, stocked with specimens of trees and animals.
>
> (WALTON 2009: 28)

Although the king's desire to create a serene environment and a visually appealing landscape ranked important to him, food production was necessary to sustain those living inside the sacred space. Fields adjacent to the temple residence were developed for cultivating food, and what was grown was offered back to the deity. Eventually, temples became the center of power in the economic, judicial, administrative, and legislative arenas — especially when it came to large-scale food production.

Wheat grain was one of the first crops in the ANE that could be cultivated and harvested on a large scale. Trees and vines didn't require the same effort. Wheat's emergence in the Fertile Crescent was a key factor in the rise of the developing world and the creation of city-states. Grain was advantageous in that it could be stored long-term — essential for large population centers, especially during times of famine. Some outside the mainstream of Egyptology have suggested that the Labyrinth (Greek for an Egyptian temple), discovered in Egypt in 1888 by Professor Flinders Petrie, was built by Joseph (Jacob's son) as a palace and granary complex. This massive compound, with over 3000 rooms, could easily have served as an administrative and economic center for food production and storage. Situated on Lake Moeris (90 km SE of Cairo), an irrigation canal connected the complex to the Nile River and watered the adjacent wheat fields. The channel is still called *Bahr Yosef* or Waterway of Joseph.

The Threshing Floor

ANE kings built temples for their gods. Each of the great cities of ancient Mesopotamia featured large temple complexes that included an inner sanctum, a ziggurat, and a sprawling garden. The temple building was the god's residence which he shared with his chosen consort. The god and his new bride entered the temple's inner chamber, sometimes called the "couch," during the annual New Year's celebration. A sacred wedding renewed the cosmic order and was followed by a seven-day temple dedication. The royal couple's union guaranteed a favorable destiny for the fertility of the land. The production of an heir was vital for bringing blessing and fruitfulness to the kingdom.

Within the temple complex was a sacred garden for planting, cultivating, and harvesting seeds that produced food for the god's household. According to Geo Widengren, "The House of the Plant of Life" (1951: 19) was a common name for temples in ANE. The garden was a field for growing food. The ziggurat, the meeting place between Heaven and Earth and where the god descended to Earth, represented the altar where food from the garden was cooked and offered up to the god.

The Holy of Holies was the inner sanctum of Jerusalem's Temple that housed the Ark of the Testimony, G-d's Word, on tablets of stone. *Yeshua* referred to the Word as seed. The Holy of Holies was represented as the storehouse, the barn, or the granary for storing seed grain. "His winnowing fork is in His hand, and He shall clear His threshing floor and gather His wheat into the barn" (Matt. 3.12). Seed grain from the threshing floor provided food for the residents inside the sacred space as well as the entire Kingdom.

Adam was a priest who worked in the field to harvest food for his family and provide offerings to his G-d. The Hebrew word for garden is *gan*. Adding the letter *resh* changes *gan* (garden) to *goren* (threshing floor). *Goren* could also mean the first place for gathering seed, which, of course, is a garden.

The One who supplies seed to the sower also provides bread for food, and He will increase your seed and will increase the yield of your righteousness.

(2 CORINTHIANS 9:10)

Yeshua often spoke of the field and equated it with the world. Many of his parables revealed the mysteries of the Kingdom couched in language related to agriculture. "The Kingdom of Heaven is like a treasure hidden in the field, which a man found and hid. And because of his joy, he goes out and sells all that he has and buys that field" (Matt. 13.44). Since the Temple complex included a "field," this is likely a reference to King David who purchased the threshing floor from Araunah as the site of the First Temple. "The field chosen by Isaac on the mountain where his father Abraham had bound him as a sacrifice would become the site of the Holy Temple, G-d's House of Prayer for all the nations" (Greenbaum, *Rejoice Reapers of the Field*). "Abraham called the temple 'mountain,' Isaac called it 'field,' Jacob called it 'palace;' this is none other than the House of G-d" (Pesikta *Rabbati* 39.5).

In the ANE, "The temple was the center of power and control from which the deity brought order to the human world. Fertility, prosperity, peace, and justice emanated from there" (Walton 2006: 127). The temple was an administrative center for food production as well. Joseph served in the most important position in ANE society, Superintendent of the Granary, which meant he was the overseer of the fields and grains. He was responsible for setting harvest dues, registering new lands in the name of the king, recording border markers, issuing land-leases, and supplying the granary with seed. There are numerous interpretations of Joseph's Egyptian name, *Tzafnat-Pa'neach*, including, "The Man to Whom Mysteries are Revealed" and "The Finder of Mysteries" (Josephus *Antiquities of the Jews* 2.6). It is also possible, that, instead of a personal name, it was a title meaning "Nourisher of Life" (Patai and Graves 1992: 263).

Anciently, the threshing floor and granary served as sacred spaces for marriage ceremonies and other temple rituals. The Egyptian god Osiris, for example, celebrated his revivification on the threshing floor of his temple. At the center of the threshing floor sat two large flat stones, one on top of the other, fitted and joined like a potter's wheel. The upper stone represented the female and the lower the male. The grinding of grain alluded to the act of marriage. When Boaz spread the corner of his robe over Ruth as she lay at his feet on the threshing floor, it was symbolic of an ANE proposal ritual (Ruth 3:9). The cover indicated Ruth's submission to Boaz as his bride, as well as his responsibility to protect her from an enemy who would seek to steal or destroy the grain harvest. The consummation of their marriage and the resulting fruit indicated a clear victory over the enemy. From Ruth came forth the line of the kings of Israel; her seed produced the royal dynasty of David — the forerunner of *the* Messiah (anointed king). "In sacred marriage ceremonies at the sanctuaries, the term 'gardener' was the epithet given to males" (George and George 2014: 134). A royal marriage that produced seed signified new creation activity and foreshadowed the reunion of Heaven and Earth and the restoration of creation.

King David understood the significance of the threshing floor. The Angel of the Lord appeared to him standing in the place "between Heaven and Earth." According to tradition, the angel stood on the Foundation Stone — the future site of the Holy of Holies where the Ark of the Covenant would sit. Both Solomon's Temple and the Second Temple that Herod expanded were constructed on Mount Moriah's foundation commonly called the *Even Shettiyah* (Foundation Stone). The threshing floor was a level, circular area — usually paved and located on a huge, flat rock on top of a mountain where the bedrock lay exposed.

David purchased the threshing floor from *Ornan* (Araunah) and set up an altar in that spot. *Ornan*, the owner of *the* most valuable piece of real estate, remains one of the truly enigmatic figures in the Bible — unique for his close relationship to the Temple. The Hebrew letters of his name suggest a possible connection to the High Priest, *Aharon*, and the Ark of the Covenant, *haAron*. Both words are formed from two words: *or* (light) and *nun* (seed) — the same letters in *Ornan's* name.

Grain was also connected to various agricultural rituals such as the first fruit offerings and the harvest festival ceremonies. The sages referred to Israel as the first of the grain. Contained within *beresheet* (in the beginning), the first word of the Bible, is the expression *bar reisheet* meaning first grain. G-d is alluding to Israel, which is called a "beginning," according to Rashi. Israel is holy to *Adonai*, the *reisheet* (first) of His crop (Jer. 2:3).

The *reisheet* or first of the wheat harvest was offered at *Shavuot* (Feast of Weeks or Pentecost) when the Second Temple was standing. Between *Pesach* (Passover) and *Shavuot* was a seven-week period filled with apprehension over the fate of the grain crop. The "closing of Passover" brought great relief to the community when the wheat harvest was finally ripe and the days of anxiety over. In Jewish tradition, *Shavuot*, "The Day of the First Fruits," coincided with the giving of the Torah seven weeks after the Exodus from Egypt. It was "the time of the wheat harvest, thereby uniting the spiritual ripening of Israel with the ripening of the wheat, and with the bringing of the offering from the field" (Hareuveni 1980: 64). Wheat grain became synonymous with righteous Israel. Joseph, who served as Pharaoh's representative, gathered and stored massive amounts of wheat grain from the fields in Egypt during the seven years of abundance. G-d promised Jacob, "I will make your seed like the sand of the sea that cannot be counted because of its abundance" (Gen. 32.13).

Yeshua the Messiah was the "first fruit" of the resurrection. In speaking of himself, he declared, "Unless a kernel of wheat falls to the ground it remains only a single seed. But if it dies, it produces many seeds" (Jn. 12:24) — righteous seed that will spread to the four corners of the earth.

During *Shavuot*, in the Second Temple, a special bread offering called *Sh'tai haLechem* (two leavened loaves) was waved before the Presence of G-d to signify a unified nation and G-d's blessing on man's earthly needs. Eating the loaves in a regal manner meant the priests sat and ate their portion of bread in the sanctified area of the Temple. Only kings descended from King David could sit in the inner courtyard; at *Shavuot*, everyone who ate was considered a "royal" priesthood and a holy nation. "To Him who loves us and has freed us from our sins by His blood and made us a Kingdom, *kohanim* to His G-d and Father" (Rev. 1.5). The Apostle Paul declared that Messiah has made us both (Jew and non-Jew) one and has broken down the middle wall of partition which previously divided. "This was done through the shedding of Messiah's blood to create in union with Himself, from the two groups, a single new humanity and thus make *shalom*" (Eph. 2:13–15).

Threshing is a process of separating the grain seed from the stalk. After the grain had been spread, yoked oxen were driven around the threshing floor to crush the stalks with their hooves. A heavy threshing board would tear the ears from the stems and loosen the grain from its husks without damaging the seed. The threshing sled bottom was covered with razor-like metal blades. Made from one piece only, its front was narrower and curved upward (thought to resemble the Ark of the Covenant).

Winnowing was the final step in the threshing process.

Once the seed was thoroughly separated from the worthless straw (stalks, husks, and any part that is not seed), the harvester scooped up the piles and tossed the grain in the air using a large fork. The wind carried away the lighter chaff as the heavier seed fell to the threshing floor to be swept up and stored in the granary.

Depictions of the threshing process stir up vivid images of the Temple. Like the threshing board, the ark cover was made from one piece of hammered gold that curved upward. The ark was G-d's throne on wheels (Ezekiel 10) and may have resembled a threshing cart. As David moved the ark by cart to the threshing floor of Nakhon, Uzzah was struck dead trying to steady it as the oxen stumbled.

G-d's portable throne on Earth, the Ark of the Covenant, sat inside the Holy of Holies called the House of the Tongues of Fire (I Enoch 14.8) — a fire that preserved the good seed (righteous Israel) while destroying the chaff (the unrighteous). A similar picture emerges: as the threshing sled was drawn over the straw and the ears, the grain escaped damage while the straw on top was trampled to pieces. "Bread grain is crushed, but not endlessly. Rumbling cart wheels and horses over it would only crush it to powder" (Is. 28.28).

G-d compares Israel, His servant, to a threshing sled that will grind up the idols which stand in the temples of the nations. The Gentile nations continually attempted to conquer Jerusalem, and in particular the Temple, to usurp G-d's throne and replace His Kingdom with theirs. They were chaff and tumbleweed that would ultimately be consumed by fire.

Then the iron, the clay, the bronze, the silver, and the gold were crushed together and became like chaff from summer threshing floors that the wind blows away. Not a trace of them can be found.

(DANIEL 2.35)

I will make you a threshing sledge, new, with sharp, double-edged spikes. You will thresh the mountains and grind them up, and will make the hills like chaff. You will winnow them, and a wind will carry them away.

(ISAIAH 41.15,16)

Therefore, as a tongue of fire consumes straw, and as chaff collapses into the flame, so their root will be like rot, and their blossom will go up like dust. For they have rejected the Torah of *Adonai Tzva'ot*, and despised the word of the Holy One of Israel.

(ISAIAH 5.24)

G-d's judgment is described as a burning flame that sets mountains/temples ablaze so the nations will know that *El Elyon* rules over the heavens and the earth. "Fire goes before Him and burns up His adversaries on every side" (Ps. 97.3). His wrath will consume the chaff, that is, nations who come against His treasured possession, Israel. He will send forth an unquenchable fire (Luke 3.17) until all the nations bow before Him and glorify His name.

Adam, Chief Gardener

The following vignette is a purely fictional account or *midrashic* story. It attempts to fill in the gaps of the biblical narrative by imagining how Adam (mankind) may have been a part of the highly civilized world of ancient Sumer. Ancient Jewish tradition often employs the art of midrash by adding missing details to the narrative in order to teach unusual concepts. The rabbis are often very aggressive in their interpretations — pushing the envelope to provide a rich, detailed description of characters and events. This was a method of teaching also used by *Yeshua*. By contrast, the Christian world generally focuses only on what is actually written in the text.

The goal here is to provide a window into the ancient Near Eastern world and to answer the question of "what if?" Could Adam have been "created" outside the garden among the pagan cultures and then brought into the garden for a particular purpose? This midrash, then, begins with Adam living in the Fertile Crescent and continues following the pattern set by Abraham when G-d called him out of Ur of the Chaldees to the promised land. The focus of the Bible is on the lineage of G-d's earthly servants, the kings (messiahs), starting with Adam and ending with the Second Adam (*Yeshua*). Therefore, Adam's "forming" may well have been an ancient coronation ceremony. "Receiving the breath" was similar to the dedication rituals the pharaohs of Egypt performed on their underlings when they were raised up to serve. Cultural descriptions cover a period from 4000–2100 BCE that reveal a flourishing civilization. During this period, the Euphrates (Greek) River was called the Buranuna.

The sun's rapid descent into the Buranuna River created a blood-like spatter stretching across the plains of the Fertile Crescent into one of the twelve city-states of Sumer known as Uruk. Excited residents hurried to the main square for the annual New Year's parade honoring the goddess, Inanna (Lady of the Sky). Her procession boasted a retinue of minor gods and goddesses, temple priests currently in service, and a host of skilled gardeners responsible for maintaining her luxuriant grounds. Chief among the gardeners was one called Adam, son of Utu (sun), whose destiny was about to unfold. Inanna was the city's patron goddess. Her smile broadened as she heard cheering from atop her perch — Uruk's only ziggurat (a man-made rectangular stepped tower that served as the connecting point between heaven and earth).

Uruk was *the* most influential city in Mesopotamia — a major hub for trade, transportation, and administration. Its heavily fortified walls, built from clay bricks, surrounded the city to protect the fields and gardens of Inanna's imposing temple complex. A series of hand-dug canals harnessed the flood waters of the Buranuna for irrigation. Many of Uruk's young men worked the gardens and lived among the priestly class in the separate district of Anu. Long days were the rule as workers labored tirelessly under the broiling Sumerian sun to provide Inanna and her royal household their daily bread. The gods had grown weary of the backbreaking work required to feed themselves and had created mankind to produce their food. The lush gardens, located on the eastern banks of the river, required constant upkeep. Human slaves became highly proficient at maintaining the opulent lifestyle of the gods. Many of the local townspeople worked in the fields growing and harvesting dates, flax, wheat, and barley. Others contributed to the tanning and pottery trades. Some of the city's residents were fortunate enough to rent land from the temple priests.

Inanna's entourage departed the city to ascend the steep steps of the seven terraces leading to her man-made mountain sanctuary. The mighty tower soared above the plains of southern Mesopotamia; from there the nobles, priests, scribes and temple officials controlled Uruk's great wealth. The entire temple complex was called Eana or House of Heaven. It included verdant gardens, a ziggurat made from fired bricks overlaid in rainbow-colored glazes, and a dazzling temple building covered with a lapis lazuli facade. Inanna, Queen of Heaven and Earth, was well known in the ancient Mesopotamian world as the Goddess of the Morning and Evening and the Light of the World. She was represented by the sycomore fig tree. As the chief lawgiver of the "Meh," the Sumerian Tablets which she stole from her father, Inanna relished her role as the Goddess of Justice. Her gift of divine wisdom and knowledge brought peace and prosperity to the people of Uruk, or so they thought.

Her horned crown proudly displayed the pine cone insignia of her sacred temple, Eana. As Uruk's chief authority over Life and Death, Inanna epitomized the essence of renewal and fertility, and so she was often identified as the Snake Goddess. Dressed in a shimmering, cobalt blue robe and bedecked in jewels of carnelian, she reflected the lower waters from which she was formed. Most evenings, she stood alone atop her sanctuary, waiting to receive her daily allotment of food from the temple priestesses.

Her temple servants fidgeted, anxious for the annual appointment of the king of Uruk. When the sun reached its zenith, the chief priest cut the liver from an unblemished sacrificial lamb. After studying its shape, color, and texture, the priest confirmed Inanna's choice. The crowd thundered its approval, and a great shout arose. Inanna entered the inner sanctuary with her loyal consort, Dumuzi — Shepherd and god of Uruk's green pastures. Their sacred mating under her *huluppu* tree ensured fertility for the land and blessings upon the city and its king. Inanna had uprooted the tree from the banks of the Buranuna and planted it in her garden. She lovingly tended to it; its resplendent trunk stretched to the sky and formed her fruitful throne. A wily serpent made its home at the root, while an Anzu built a nest in the tree's crown.

In seven days, the newly appointed sovereign would enter the inner sanctum with the goddess's specially appointed high priestess, Entu, as part of the coronation ritual. Inanna would present the garments of kingship and offer the holy crown to the new king when he sat on the throne. The high priestess would pick the sacred fruit from the *huluppu*, eat it, and then present it to the suzerain. He would be raised up to become divine — ceremonially "born again" to heavenly parents, Inanna and Dumuzi. The king would emerge from the inner chamber as Inanna's image-bearer — the godly offspring and precious fruit of her womb.

At his coronation, the divine ruler entered the eternal world of the gods through the regenerative powers of Inanna. Eating the fruit also meant he received Inanna's wisdom and knowledge to govern the kingdom. Each day, he was given instruction in mathematics, astronomy, and medicine — which enabled him to mediate as high priest between her House of Heaven and the city of Uruk.

> Uruk, the god's handiwork, and Eana, a house
> come down from heaven,
> whose parts were fashioned by the great gods.
> Its great wall, a cloud standing on the ground.
> The august abode established by An is entrusted to you,
> You are the king and warrior.

The king was also responsible for securing all legal documents — including official letters, contracts, economic records, and Uruk's literary and religious texts. They were carefully organized and signed with royal cylinder seals made from materials such as ivory, bone, or wood. The stamps, which represented the sovereign's signature and his identity, were carefully stored in the Chamber of the Treasury inside Inanna's temple.

Inanna spotted the chief gardener, Adam, standing alone near the ziggurat's monumental staircase. Knowing he had served with distinction in Eana, the royal House of Heaven, Innana considered him a qualified candidate for King of Uruk. And so, through divination, Innana examined the stars and constellations for the celestial sign. She was thrilled to see the moon making its eclipse and interpreted this omen as her confirmation of the appointment of Adam, Son of Utu, as the next ruler. His enthronement ceremony was set for seven days.

Adam, exhausted from working in the fields, plopped down under the shade of a giant sycamore fig to escape the sweltering heat. He reflected on his service, his meteoric rise to chief gardener, and now...the highest office in the land — second only to the goddess Inanna! His new title had a magical sound: Adam, King of Uruk! His enthusiasm soon wore thin when he considered the daunting task of governing the people. Managing the capricious nature of the goddess could prove intolerable. Adam had often dreamed of a different life beyond the borders of Uruk in which the gods were honorable and fair and justice and mercy ruled. He wondered aloud if he would be willing to abandon his dream in order to serve as royal ruler of Uruk.

Adam leaped to his feet; an angel, cloaked in brilliant light with fiery eyes burning like torches, appeared before him. In a thundering voice, the angel implored him to leave the city immediately for an unknown land in the mountains near the Great Sea. Unnerved, Adam raced down the steep slope to the city. Darting in and out of alleyways, glancing over his shoulder, he slipped into his house unnoticed. After collecting a few belongings, he changed into a fresh sheepskin shirt and plotted his escape.

Adam crisscrossed the vast network of canals connecting the city to the river and made his way to Uruk's main port. The docks were bustling with activity. Ships moving goods and people, upstream and downstream, revealed a flourishing maritime industry — the envy of the known world. The city-state had become prosperous from its trade in jewelry, wine, and food — especially barley and wheat which grew in Uruk's rich soil. Adam hired a local who owned a small, reed sailboat to take him upstream to the city of Mari. Its sails, woven papyri mats placed between pairs of poles, were superior for navigation. The boat, which resembled an over-sized wicker basket, was coated with bitumen to prevent leaks. Adam tried in vain to make himself comfortable inside the cramped hull.

For the inhabitants of the Fertile Crescent, the River was a divinity to be worshipped. The voyage across symbolized a supernatural journey — a metaphor for entering the inaccessible place called the afterlife. The River was the pathway to the underworld and an impenetrable boundary; crossing it would forever alter the individual. Adam remained apprehensive. Did this mean instant death? Was this truly a path of no return? He knew the underworld was a "house" from which no one ever left.

The boatman signaled to Adam as the city of Mari came into view. Located just west of the Buranuna, Mari was centrally located on the trade route between Sumer in the south and the Levant in the west. It was the first planned city in the region — designed with an inner ring to defend against foreign invaders and an outer ring to protect the city from floods. Engineers took advantage of its unique location and dug a canal that circumvented the double bend in the river. Trading ships could easily bypass the winding river and sail straight ahead. Mari's numerous canals allowed the city control over its entry points and provided huge profits from tolls charged to ships passing through. Mari, known as a copper smelting center, produced terra cotta figurines that resembled the local gods and goddesses.

After settling with the boatman, Adam hired a donkey from Mari's central square for the overland journey. His first stop was Tadmor, the great trading hub, located halfway between the Great Sea and the Buranuna. Adam relaxed at the city's popular oasis and watched with fascination as a steady throng of merchants transported their goods to market. Long considered a cultural crossroads, Tadmor was the central station for commercial caravansaries and a meeting place for diplomatic delegations. From there, Adam traveled west, around the southern edge of the snow-capped peaks of Mount Hermon, to cross the surging waters of the upper Jordan. At Dan, he entered through an enormous triple-gated complex constructed of sun-dried bricks. Adam was surprised by the verdant landscape — coral and lavender colored flowers blanketed the river's edge. He refreshed himself in the sparkling waters and stretched out to bask in the warmth of the afternoon sun.

At last, he reached the trio of mountains — the destination of his new home. As he began the grueling ascent, the angel of the Lord appeared and led him to the heavenly mountain retreat known as "Heaven and Earth." A sweet perfume filled his nose as he passed the towering mud-brick wall that hid a garden sanctuary. As the former chief gardener in Uruk, Adam could hardly wait to enter this mountain paradise. A large, hewn stone at the entrance to the city proudly displayed the name: *Urusalim* (the foundation of *Shalem*). The Angel of the Lord had called it *Yerush Shalem*, the Inheritance of Peace. Clearly it was not a city built by the hands of human slaves like the grand temple complexes of Mesopotamia.

As Adam ascended, he observed the predominately two-storied, flat-roofed houses built on limestone bedrock — so different from the dwellings of the alluvial plains of Mesopotamia. The city's main square was buzzing with commercial activity. Market stalls were filled with merchandise — mostly durable pottery suited for their agrarian lifestyle. The ceramic vessels were made from the region's native clay. Local artisans first removed the stones and excess debris from the clay then added water before throwing it on the potter's wheel. The wheel was a simple, horizontal, revolving tablet made from two flat stones that resembled birthing stones; one rotated on top of the other. Before the earthenware pots were fired and painted ebony, distinctive geometric designs were cut into the clay. The market stalls were also filled with terra cotta figurines, like those in Mari, as well as a plethora of copper tools: chisels, polished axes, and small sickle blades for harvesting crops — essential for the burgeoning agricultural trade.

As Adam finished unpacking his belongings, a courtier from the royal household summoned him to appear before the ruler of *Yerush Shalem*. *Melech Zedekiah* (King of the Righteous) and his wife *Chacham* (Wisdom), the Great Lady of the household, ruled the city-state and served as ambassadors to the One True G-d. *Melech Zedekiah* built an official royal residence patterned after the heavens in which the king displayed his impressive skills in cultivating the palace gardens. Some noted his expertise in horticulture far exceeded his abilities on the battlefield.

The Coronation

Heaven is my throne, and the earth is my footstool. Where then is the house you would build for me? Where is the place of My rest?

(ISAIAH 66.1)

Adam discovered a garden paradise in the land by the Great Sea, not completely unlike the temples and gardens of the east. However, no ziggurats rose above the plains for "the gods" to descend from Heaven to Earth, nor were there any human slaves to clothe, feed, and nurture the gods. Instead, this sanctuary was the mountain where the eternal G-d dwelled "in the midst" of His creation — the center and connecting point of His Cosmic Temple.

The One True G-d had blessed *Melech Zedekiah* with wisdom and knowledge to build a grand palace with lavish gardens on the top of the mountain. A serrated, emerald peak punctured the sky as rivers of living water poured out through a celestial spout cutting creases into the mountain's limestone rock. The water funneled down through colonnaded aqueducts then surged over rocky outcroppings to empty into a deep, crystal pool. A sapphire mist embraced the rocks; its tentacles hovered along primordial pathways as if suspended in time. Massive obsidian pillars supported quadrangular arches to provide shade for the walkways underneath. Stairways carpeted in brilliant light reached up to multi-tiered platforms that showcased a profusion of trees, shrubs, and vines. Pearls of dew blanketed tender shoots; reed grasses vibrated loudly — amplifying Heaven's woodwind ensemble. Galleries of translucent roses displayed their watercolor canvases. Scented bouquets of ambrosia wafted through the sacred space adding to the exotic, botanical feast.

In the center of the garden stood two trees — stately pillars that connected Heaven to Earth and served as the cosmic axis and nucleus for the world. Two cherubim provided protection.

The trees sprouted up from the ground near the Gihon spring; their deep roots drank from the eternal fountain. The Tree of Life appeared as a flame of fire with ornamental, bronze-colored knobs dotting the gold trunk and thick branches in glowing hues of burnt sienna. White, feathered flowers with topaz centers bloomed in loose clusters on its limbs. The tough, lanceolate-shaped, leathery leaves possessed healing powers. Luscious fruit produced a rich, virgin oil used for anointing kings with Godly Wisdom.

The immense canopy from the Tree of the Knowledge of Good and Evil provided pleasant shade. Bright, emerald leaves were filled with a milky, latex sap that protected the tree and irritated human flesh. The tree's roots descended along the gnarly trunk to form a gilded latticework. Muscular branches produced beams perfect for framing a house. The early, bronze-skinned fruit, tinged with a lavender hue, contained a white ring of seeds surrounded by a mass of jelly-like flesh. It was the sweetest delicacy in the garden.

Residents of *Yerush Shalem* awoke to brilliant, blue skies on coronation day — the annual New Year's festival. Clutching their leafy boughs, they lined the grand plaza outside *Melech Zedekiah's* palace. Some arranged their palm and olive branches over the stone-paved street. An elite unit of the royal guard, dressed in full regalia, exited first from the palace's main gate. Royal pages followed behind with torches blazing. Noblemen carried tribute for the newly crowned king: gold, frankincense, and myrrh. Palace servants closed ranks — weighed down with food and drink for the royal banquet to follow. Ladies of the queen's household, adorned in fine jewels, rode the suzerain's horses. Finally, the future king appeared. A shout of acclamation arose. Adam nodded his approval to the spectators as he rode past on *Melech Zedekiah's* donkey. He carried with him the insignia of power — a royal *ketonet* (long sleeved robe) laced with threads of gold and silver and woven with the royal colors: blue, scarlet, and purple. Adam clenched his staff specially made for the event.

The crowd erupted in shouts of *"haMelech, Ben Adam — baruch haba b'shem Adonai!"* (The king, Son of Man — blessed is He who comes in the name of the Lord). The royal entourage passed the crowd before beginning their descent along the well-traveled path to the Gihon Spring in the valley below — a sacred spot that featured the spring known as the "fountain of living water." Crystal-clear waters bubbled up intermittently from deep inside the subterranean cavern — the lifeblood of the city and the location for the investiture and anointing. Each time the cave filled with water, the overflow emptied through a split in the rocks. An adjacent pool collected water for the royal *mikvah*.

The first part of the ceremony — the investiture, the anointing, and the acclamation — took place at the Gihon. The second part (which included assuming a new title, taking up the throne, and receiving homage from palace officials) would be celebrated in Eden: the throne room of G-d. As the adopted son of the Eternal King, Adam's new name would be *Ben Elohim*, Son of G-d. His dual position as high priest and sovereign signified that he would be *the* image-bearer of *Elohim*. Eating fruit from the Tree of Life would secure his eternal status. (Adam, however, would never be enthroned in Eden. In time, a second Adam would be raised up to become the immortal, divine ruler — *Ben Elohim*, Son of G-d. The second Adam would defeat G-d's enemies, bring rest to the cosmos, restore the Kingdom of Heaven, and sit at the right hand of G-d.)

Adam immersed in the living waters of the Gihon for ritual purification. Water drawn from a distinctive, gold vessel was poured out onto the *adamah* (ground). Adam was "formed" from this moistened clod of earth into the image of the master potter. The earth, called *adamah*, bowed in honor of *Ben Adam* (Son of Man) — G-d's priestly representative in the garden.

A blast from the ram's horn announced the anointing.

Melech Zedekiah took another ram's horn filled with freshly pressed olive oil from the Tree of Life and anointed him with divine Wisdom. The rich oil saturated his head and trickled down over his beard onto the collar of his royal *ketonet*. Adam received the *ruach* — Wisdom from the one who breathes life into the nostrils. A silhouetted new moon served as the ceremony's silent witness. The foundations of the earth shook. The new king was declared Anointed One — Messiah.

Adam blessed the One True G-d in the presence of the royal court and shouted, "Yours is the greatness, the strength, the splendor, the triumph, and the glory — everything in Heaven and Earth. Yours is the Kingdom and the sovereignty over every leader. Wealth and honor come from you, and you rule everything — in your hand is power and strength, and it is in your hand to make anyone great or strong."

Adam accepted the royal *eduth* written by the hand of G-d: a written decree that recognized the king's authority and outlined the protocol for entering Eden. Faithfully serving the One True G-d meant Adam could not eat fruit from the Tree of the Knowledge of Good and Evil. Eating its fruit barred the king from entering the realm of the divine in Eden. The tree was *kedushah* — holy and set apart. Its fruit was declared *orlah*, forbidden, for three years. If he ate it, Adam would be exiled from the garden and would then grow plants in a field filled with thistles, thorns, and briars.

The coronation ceremony continued. Adam saw heaven split, and the eternal sanctuary appeared at the firmament's portal — a Holy House arrayed in dazzling gold like a bride clothed with the rays of the sun and wearing a crown of stars. An angel exited the eastern gate and stood before Adam with a message from G-d's oracle. An *eshah*, a wife, would serve alongside Adam as an *ahzer*, "one who helped," to build his house. She would be an ally to Adam and his equal. From her "garden," fruit would come forth and extend righteousness and justice to the world.

G-d separated *Chavah* from Adam and set her apart for priestly duty. A heavenly tabernacle on Earth, her bones were interlocking wooden beams, and her flesh red-dyed, ram skins that covered the holy dwelling place. Arrayed in fine linen and purple, *Chavah* and her husband received respect at the garden gate where they sat to judge with the host of Heaven. Supreme honor was bestowed upon Adam and *Chavah*, and they were bursting with hope and high expectations for their future seed.

✡   ✡   ✡

Of G-ds and Kings

Yet G-d is my King of old, working salvation in the midst
of the land. You split the sea with your power. You
smashed the monsters' heads in the water.

(PSALM 74.12,13)

The language of "kingship" permeates the Bible; the Temple serves as the backdrop. The ANE world was organized around the divine ruler who participated in bringing forth the world at the first creation. Ancient kings, when enthroned, became the royal image of the deity. When the sovereign entered the temple, he became the idol of his god — a statue made by human hands. In the ancient Near East, the king was thought to be "in the image" of his god. As *the* concrete symbol of the deity's rulership, the king exercised his sovereign authority over the empire from the temple.

In Mesopotamia, the king's ascent to the throne was understood as an adoption ritual. Called "son of god," the divine ruler functioned in a predominantly political and bureaucratic setting. He was the god's special servant endowed with divine wisdom to expand the kingdom to the four corners of the earth (Nebuchadnezzar's rule in Daniel 4).

It is you, O king! For you have grown great and mighty. Your greatness reaches to heaven, and your authority extends to the end of the earth.

(DANIEL 4.19)

The temple of the god was likened to a garden and a world mountain; the king was the garden's *axis mundi* — a vertical pillar or world tree that connected Heaven to Earth.

His temple was a tall mountain whose summit resembles the throne of G-d where the eternal King will sit when he descends to visit the earth with goodness. As far as the fragrant tree, not a single human has the authority to touch it until the great judgment. And the elect will be presented with its fruit for life.

(1 ENOCH 25.3–5)

The garden was sacred space called Paradise, cultivated by the gardener king, that served as the portal through which he could communicate directly with the deity. Ephrem's Hymns (written in the mid-fourth Century CE) describe Paradise as a "mountain divided into three levels, the lowest for penitents, the middle for the righteous, and the highest for the triumphant" (Hymn 2.11). "The assembly of the Saints bears resemblance to Paradise; in it, each day is plucked the fruit of Him who gives life to all" (Hymn 6.8).

Ultimately, the garden embodied the ideal state of harmony achieved by a successful ruler/gardener under the authority of his god. In the *Legend of Sargon* (Sargon means the King is Legitimate), a parallel with the birth of Moses and his position in Pharaoh's house is evident. "I told of a birth legend — son of a priestess, abandoned by mother at a local river, rescuers and raised by the adoptive father who set him to become a gardener — his services as gardener were pleasing to Ishtar and he became king" (*Legend of Sargon*, 11.11–13).

In ANE traditions there was the garden of paradise where a gardener supervises the Tree of Life growing at the Water of Life, a tree from whose branches he has taken a twig which he carries as his rod or scepter.

(BARKER 2008: 93)

According to Geo Widengren, a "Tree of Life was a mythical ritual symbol of both god and king" (1951: 42). Daniel portrays King Nebuchadnezzar this way. Ezekiel describes the King of Assyria using similar language that is taken from Eden.

The tree that you saw grow large and strong, whose top reached to heaven and that was visible to all the earth, whose leaves were beautiful and whose fruit was so abundant that there was food for all in it and beneath which the beasts of the field lived and in its branches birds of the sky dwelt.

(DANIEL 4.18)

Behold, Assyria was a cedar in Lebanon, with beautiful branches shadowing the forest, of loft height. Water nourished it, the deep made it tall, with its rivers going around its planting as it sent out its water-courses to all the trees of the field. Therefore, its height was loftier than all the trees of the field. All great nations lived under its shade. The cedars in the garden of G-d could not compare with it.

(EZEKIEL 31.3–6,8)

The trunk of the tree, compared to a human spinal column, was the king who represented, "an angelic being, the high priest, and the central shaft of the *menorah* which symbolizes the Presence of G-d" (Barker 2008: 94). John saw one like a Son of Man clothed in a robe (*ketonet*) down to his feet with a golden belt wrapped around his chest and standing in the "midst" of the seven golden *menorot* (Rev. 1.13).

In Jerusalem, the tree of Jesse was Israel's royal house from which the anointed branch would bear fruit (Is. 11.1). The *Tzemach* or righteous sprout, beautiful and glorious, was a title for the Messiah (Is. 4.2). "A man whose Name is the *Tzemach* will branch out from his place and build the Temple of *Adonai*. He will build the Temple. He will bear splendor and sit and rule on His throne" (Zech. 6.12,13). Trees sprouting indicated the perpetuation of the dynasty. In the first century, believers saw themselves not only as righteous branches connected to the true vine (Messiah, the king) but also as a new creation (sprout), a Kingdom of priests, called the Sons of G-d (based on Messiah's title, Son of G-d). They were heavenly priests enjoying life in an eternal Kingdom on Earth while at the same time living in the world.

For Israel, the divine ruler was G-d's "raised up" servant — filled with the Spirit. "The anointed king was the bond of the eternal covenant which held all things in their appointed place" (Barker 2008: 103). The Prophet Samuel anointed King Saul by pouring a vial of oil on his head, "Has *Adonai* not anointed you ruler over His inheritance…Then the *Ruach* of *Adonai* will seize you and you will prophesy with them — you will turn into another man" (1 Sam. 10.6). David's last words are confirmation: "the utterance of the man raised on high, the anointed of the G-d of Jacob and the sweet singer of Israel: The *Ruach Adonai* has spoken through me and His word is on my tongue" (2 Sam. 23.1–2). The sovereign was the man chosen by G-d, enthroned (raised up) and given the title, "Son of G-d." He was "an earthly king, a heavenly patron, and an angelic being," and so the "divine status of the king was part of the temple cult" (Barker 2008: 73).

I will raise up your seed, who will come forth from you (your body) after you, and I will establish his kingdom.

He will build a house for My Name, and I will establish his royal throne forever. I will be a father to him, and he will be a son to Me...so your house and your kingship will be secure forever before you; your throne will be established forever.

(2 SAMUEL. 7.11–13,16)

I rested on the Spirit of the Lord; and the Spirit raised me on high: and made me stand on my feet in the height of the Lord, before his perfection and his glory, while I was praising him by the composition of his songs. The Spirit brought me forth before the face of the Lord; and although a son of man, I was named Illuminate, the Son of G-d...For according to the greatness of the Most High, so he made me: and like his own newness he renewed me: and he anointed me from his own perfection.

(ODES OF SOLOMON 36)

Israel's ideal king established his rule on a foundation of righteousness and justice. He was given direct access to G-d's oracle to receive the instruction needed to govern the people justly and to serve as an open channel for the nation's blessings. A godless ruler meant disaster for the people.

Also a priest, the king officiated sacrifices and offerings, and he mediated on behalf of the people. G-d's power and authority were exercised through the king who was His image-bearer. Filled with Wisdom, the sovereign also shared in *Adonai's* divine qualities: life, eternity, splendor, glory, and majesty. His sin became the people's sin; his righteousness was their righteousness. As the visible image of the invisible G-d, Israel's ruler was described as the firstborn of all creation (Col. 1.15).

I have found David My servant. With my holy oil, I have anointed him...He will call to Me: You are My Father, my

G-d and the rock of my salvation. I also will set him as firstborn — the highest of the kings of earth...His seed I will establish forever, and his throne as the days of heaven.

(PSALM 89.21,27–29)

Adam's position, before he violated the commandment not to eat from the Tree of the Knowledge of Good and Evil, was that of firstborn of creation. As the representative of mankind, his position would eventually be restored when *Yeshua*, the Messiah's image-bearing vocation, unfolded before those who would become a "new creation." Described as his chosen image-bearers and the Sons of G-d, his gardeners would once again cultivate fruit trees and serve as his royal priesthood.

For like the days of a tree, so will be the days of My people, and My chosen ones will long enjoy the work of their hands. They will not labor in vain nor bear children for calamity. For they are the offspring of those blessed by *Adonai*, as well as descendants with them.

(ISAIAH 65.22B,23)

CHAPTER TWO

THE GARDEN

The earth is Adonai's and all that fills it — the world,
and those dwelling on it. For He founded it upon
the seas, and established it upon the rivers.
Who may go up on the mountain
of Adonai? Who may stand in His Holy Place?
One with clean hands and a pure heart.
(Psalm 24.1–4a)

G-d formed His Cosmic House into three domains: Heaven, Earth, and Sea. The waters below covered the earthly Temple, so it appeared empty and without form. On the third day, the seas gathered; Earth, now visible, became the center of the cosmos. Foundations were laid for three courtyards: Eden, the garden, and the field. Molded and shaped by the potter's hand, the earthly Temple transformed into an enormous mountain that bound Heaven and Earth together. Bolts of lightning stabbed the skies. His Word thundered. The mountain shook violently as torrents of fire streamed from its summit. Heavenly wisdom bubbled up from the fountain of living water; it cascaded over craggy rocks then flowed into the garden to water the profusion of trees.

✡   ✡   ✡

Heaven, Earth, and Sea were part of a tripartite architectural structure that formed G-d's cosmic Temple. Earth was its sacred center. Various elements were connected to the center: a cosmic mountain, rivers that flowed from the summit, and a garden of trees. The Garden of Eden was designed in a tripartite structure with an inner chamber to the west, a garden to the east, and a field beyond the garden. According to John Walton, Eden and its adjoining garden formed two distinct regions (2001: 167–168). He compared Eden to the Holy of Holies and the garden to the Holy Place in the Temple (182–183). The rabbis also recognized a distinction between Eden and the garden (BT *Ta'anit* 10a). R. Samuel ben *Nahamani* declared, "This is Eden, which has never been seen by the eye of any creature, perhaps you will say, where then was Adam? He was in the garden. Perhaps you will say, the garden and Eden are the same? NOT SO!" (BT *Berachot* 34b).

Eden mirrored the heavenly realm; it was an invisible world beyond time that corresponded to the Holy of Holies in the Temple. "Eden is not in space and time, but is the ever-present ideal, the beyond" (Barker 2008: 103). Walton said Eden was *the* source for creation's waters and housed G-d's palatial estate; the garden then adjoined His residence (2009: 27–28). According to G. Anderson, "Eden, as a luxuriant cosmic mountain becomes an archetype or symbol for the earthly Temple" (1988: 192–99). The prophet Isaiah described Eden as "the mountain of the Lord's house" (Is. 2:2).

G-d imparted justice to the world from His throne in Eden. In the Temple, the Holy of Holies, or inner sanctum, housed the Ark of the Testimony. Also called the *debir*, meaning word or oracle, it was where G-d spoke to His anointed servants. Eden is formed from two Hebrew words: *ahd* (witness or testimony) and *din* (judge). In ancient times, a judge sat in the gate of the city where he convened court, adjudicated cases, and brought life to the community. A variation of *ahd* is *edut*, which were royal decrees written on a scroll that a king received at his inauguration. These decrees were foundational for governing the kingdom. The king was to exercise justice, mercy, and truth. The word *ehd* (mist) is also the root of *edut*. "The *mist* that went up from the earth and watered the face of the ground" (Gen. 2.6). The Temple on Zion was a well-watered garden and a spring that never fails (Is. 58.11). Adding the letter *nun* (seed) to *ehd* (mist) forms Eden — the place where water and seed originated. From G-d's Holy mountain in Jerusalem, which represented Eden, His *edut* (law or word) went forth like a river to bring justice to the nations.

For as the earth brings forth its sprouts, and as a garden causes things sown to spring up, so *Adonai Elohim* will cause justice and praise to spring up before all the nations.

(ISAIAH 61.11)

According to G.K. Beale, the Tree of the Knowledge of Good and Evil likely functioned as a judgment tree: "The place where Adam should have gone to 'discern between good and evil,' and thus where he should have judged the serpent as 'evil' and pronounced judgment on it, as it entered the Garden." (2008: 129). Additionally, "the discerning between good and evil is a Hebrew expression that refers to kings or authoritative figures being able to make judgments in carrying out justice" (128). Beale also stated, "the ark in the Holy of Holies, which contained the law (which led to wisdom), echoes the tree of the knowledge of good and evil" (which also led to wisdom). Other scholars suggest the tree foreshadowed the two stone tablets inside the Ark of the Covenant. "Both the touching of the ark and the partaking of the tree's fruit result in death" (Beale and Kim 2014: 18).

The heavenly veil that separated Eden from the garden sanctuary was linked to the firmament. In the Tabernacle, a curtain of blue, scarlet, purple, and fine white linen, woven with cherubim, separated the Holy of Holies (Eden) from the Holy Place (garden). Ephrem the Syrian said that the Tree of the Knowledge of Good and Evil was like the curtain of the Temple, and the Tree of Life was the Holy of Holies. The book of Enoch suggests the Tree of Life would be transplanted from Eden's summit to the garden below (1 Enoch 24–25).

In the Second Temple, the high priest passed through a corridor between two curtains before entering the Holy of Holies on the Day of Atonement. On five separate occasions, he entered the inner chamber to perform atonement rituals that included sprinkling the blood of bulls and goats over the Ark of the Covenant and on the curtain, as well as placing incense on a shovelful of hot coals. Clothed in fine, white linen garments, he appeared as the Angel of the Lord draped in robes of white light standing before G-d's throne. The incense ritual was part of repairing the breach in the Eternal Covenant. The incense smoke ascending in a column re-connected the people to their G-d (Rev. 8.3). Symbolically, the blood and the incense forgave sin, cleansed and restored the Temple and the nation, and re-established unity between Heaven and Earth.

The Garden

The visible and invisible worlds merged in the garden (the Holy Place) — the sacred center between Eden and the field. Margaret Barker suggests the garden paradise was located in between corruptibility and incorruptibility. G.K. Beale said the garden, separated from the outer world, is where "G-d's priestly servant worships G-d by obeying him, by cultivating, and by guarding" (2004: 75).

The ritual ceremonies carried out by the priests in the Holy Place inside the Temple symbolically restored creation (similar to the high priest in the Holy of Holies) by uniting Heaven with Earth. Barker said this meant bringing the prayers and repentance of the people to G-d and the blessing and Presence of G-d out to the people.

The king-priest extended his rule by bringing order to the earthly realm from the center of the garden, which was at the source of creation. G-d "resting" Adam in the garden (Gen. 2.15) was a sign that the earth had been subdued and freed from chaos. With the aid of the royal *edut* (decrees), Adam's service brought stability to the world. As the chief gardener and the first of the royal tent keepers, Adam exercised his priestly vocation in bearing fruit. The Qumran community identified itself as the Temple of Adam — an Eden of glory like a garden bearing fruit and an everlasting planting (Beale 2004: 78).

"The Aramaic translation of Genesis 2.15 (Targum *Neofiti*) underscores this priestly notion of Adam explaining that he was placed in the garden 'to toil in the Law and to observe its commandments'" (70). Fretheim connected keeping the soil with keeping the commandments just as a king kept the *edut*. In the Dead Sea Scrolls (4Q418), Adam's descendants "who will obey" are described as "walking in an eternal plantation" (13,14). "The main task of this vocation is 'image-bearing' reflecting the Creator's wise stewardship into the world and reflecting the praises of all creation back to its maker. Those who do so are the 'royal priesthood,' and the 'kingdom of priests,' the people who are called to stand at the dangerous but exhilarating point where heaven and earth meet" (Wright 2016: 76). In the book of Revelation, the twenty-four elders sing a new song as *kohanim* (priests) who reign over the earth (5.10). The context is the restored cosmos, the new creation, in which "New Covenant" image-bearers work as divine gardeners on G-d's holy mountain: The Temple.

When serving inside the Holy Place, the high priest wore garments woven of fine white linen embroidered with blue, scarlet, and purple that matched the inner curtain before the Holy of Holies. "Now the vestment of the high priest being made of linen signified the earth; the blue denoted the sky. [G-d] also appointed the breastplate to be placed in the middle of the ephod, to resemble the earth, for that, has the very middle place of the world" (Josephus *Antiquities* 3.184–5). Philo described the high priest's garments worn in the Holy Place as a copy of the universe (Special laws I.84–7). An outer curtain, hanging at the entrance to the Holy Place (likely the curtain that tore at *Yeshua's* death) depicted images of a starry sky. Called the "Babylonian tapestry" in the Second Temple, it was "embroidered of blue and fine linen, of scarlet also, and purple wrought with marvelous skill. Nor was this mixture of materials without its mystical interpretation, but was a kind of image of the universe" (Josephus *The Jewish War* 5.212–14).

According to A. Pelletier, the purpose for the veil was to obscure from view of the public the mystery of the abode of G-d and to reserve it for the privileged priesthood. The veil's needlework was reminiscent of the garden sanctuary. "This veil was very ornamental and embroidered with all sorts of flowers which the earth produces" (Josephus *Antiquities* 3.124,126). Barker suggests the curtain that separated the two worlds was the incarnate flesh or Presence of G-d in material form on earth — adding that both *Yeshua's* flesh and the veil were torn at his death (2008: 105).

Isaiah cried out for the restoration of Heaven and Earth. "Oh, that you would rend [to tear like a garment] the heavens and come down, that the mountains [worldly kingdoms] might quake and tremble at your Presence" (Is. 63.19b). The Kingdom Temple is represented by a high mountain filling the earth, a mighty tree whose top reaches into the heavens, a garden overflowing with trees of succulent fruit, a vineyard bursting with juicy clusters of grapes, and whitened fields of wheat grain ready for harvest. *Yeshua* described the Kingdom as here now but not yet — a garden that is present but unseen. He chose to reveal the Kingdom using agricultural images — the language of a fruitful garden sanctuary. Parables describe fertile soil, seed grain, buried treasure, mighty trees, vineyards, threshing floors, and storehouses. Kingdom workers (who are priests) were sowers of seed, horticulturists, wheat farmers, and laborers in orchards.

Yeshua's parables are *midrashic* stories that communicate how the Kingdom functions: sowing seed in good soil (Matt. 13.18–23), finding hidden treasure in a field (Matt. 13.34), or a man hiring workers for his vineyard (Matt. 20.1–15). The Kingdom is compared to a mustard seed which a man took and planted in his field. "It grew and became a [cosmic] tree and the birds of the air nested in its branches" (Matt. 13.32). When kings in the ancient world routed an enemy, they often took the seeds and tree saplings from the defeated ruler's garden to plant in their gardens. Birds of the air referred to the king's subjects. Seed-bearing plants and fruit-producing trees were metaphors for human priests and kings formed in G-d's image. The parables are new creation language based on the pattern of the original creation.

Yeshua explained the hidden meaning of the Kingdom to his disciples, for they had eyes to see, ears to hear, and hearts to receive. "To you has been given to know the secrets of the Kingdom of Heaven, but to them, it has not been given" (13.11). "[The Kingdom] will not come by waiting for it, it will not be a matter of saying 'here it is,' rather the Kingdom is spread out upon the earth and men do not see it." (Gospel of Thomas 113). For *Yeshua's* disciples, the Kingdom/garden was a fully functioning, visible reality. For those on the outside — the deaf, the blind, and the stiff-necked — the garden remained hidden until they were ready to receive it.

Yeshua announced he was the true vine and that his Father was the vinedresser (Jn. 15.1). A reference from Isaiah depicts

G-d as the master gardener planting a vine in His vineyard: "My beloved had a vineyard on a very fertile hill, dug it out and cleared its stones, planted with a choice vine and built a tower in the midst..." (Is. 5.1,2). Towers or elevated shelters (in vineyards) were transformed into the family's summer residence with sleeping quarters. From this vantage point, they could watch over their crops until harvest time. These were small shelters constructed of large stones with branches laid out on the roofs to resemble *sukkahs* (temporary huts used during the week-long Feast of Tabernacles) — like the priests on duty in the Temple sleeping in their dormitories during their weekly rotations. Imagery of the priests guarding G-d's vineyard also emerges. "In that day sing to her, a vineyard of delight! I, *Adonai* watch over it, I water it every moment. I guard it day and night so that no one may harm it" (27.3).

G-d planted his anointed king [Messiah], the vine, in the center of His vineyard — the place where Heaven and Earth meet. *Yeshua* tells the parable of a "man" who planted a vineyard (Mk. 12.1–11, Luke 20.9–19). It is likely a reference to Noah who planted a vineyard after exiting the ark (the ark was the Temple suspended between Heaven and Earth). Noah's name means rest or comfort — a hint of his king-like status. In the ANE, "rest" indicated enemies had been subdued (i.e. the flood had dissipated), the king was enthroned, and the Kingdom had become operational. As high priest and king, Noah would provide comfort, or more accurately, repentance, in the place where sins were forgiven: the temple. Unfortunately, Noah, the "man," brought shame upon the sacred space by exposing his nakedness. This expression came to be a euphemism for exile.

The parable describes a man constructing a hedge of stones around the vineyard, digging a pit for the winepress, and building a guard tower. The "man" leases the vineyard (temple) to tenant farmers (chief priests) and leaves on a journey. After sending numerous servants in his place, who are either beaten or killed, the "man" sends his "beloved son" and heir to collect the vineyard's fruit. He, too, is killed by the tenant farmers. "The master of the vineyard [G-d] will come and destroy those tenants and give the vineyard [inheritance] to others" (Luke 20.9–19). The others are His image-bearing priests who have repented and turned from idolatry.

Yeshua railed against the elitist Temple leadership for contaminating the sacred space with their idolatry. He compared them to the tenant farmers. Some of the chief priests, under Annas the High Priest, aligned themselves with Herod, Pilate, and Rome. Seeking after personal gain, the ruling authorities placed heavy burdens on the people instead of providing "comfort" in the place where sins were forgiven.

Garden Furniture

When the pilgrims arrived at the Temple for the agricultural festivals, the Babylonian tapestry was pulled back enabling them to see inside the Holy Place. This curtain was rent at *Yeshua's* death. "At the festivals, to accommodate the large crowds, all Israelites were permitted to enter the priests' hall on which occasion the curtain of the vestibule was raised to show the people the interior of the *Hekhal* (Holy Place). The people, though tightly packed, could find sufficient space in which to prostrate themselves, this being one of the miracles associated with the Temple" (Jewish Encyclopedia Online: *Temple Administration and Service*). The curtain being raised in the Temple at festivals was significant. It meant the people who were bringing the bounty from the land could *see* the reality of the Kingdom inside the Holy Place.

✡   ✡   ✡

Three pieces of furniture: the seven-branched menorah, the incense altar, and the table of the Bread of the Presence reveal how the Kingdom functions. All three originated inside the Ark of the Covenant but were set in the Holy Place. The *menorah* corresponded to Aaron's rod that budded, the Bread of the Faces was the manna inside the golden jar, and the Altar of Incense connected to the tablets of the covenant.

> Now even the first one had regulations for worship and the earthly sanctuary. For a tent was prepared: in the outer part were the menorah, the table and the presentation of the bread — this is called the Holy Place. Beyond the second curtain was a dwelling called the Holy of Holies.... in the ark was a golden jar holding the manna, Aaron's rod that budded, and the tablets of the covenant — and above it, cherubim of glory overshadowing the mercy seat.
>
> (HEBREWS 9.1–7)

The table for the Bread of the Faces, or Presence, stood at the right hand of the priests, directly across from the *menorah*, as they entered the Holy Place. Like the Ark of the Covenant, the table was made from acacia wood and overlaid with gold. Rings were attached to the four corners so poles could be inserted for easy transport. The bread, considered "the most sacred of all offerings," (Targum *Onkelos* Lev. 24.9) symbolized the Presence of G-d in the sanctuary. Twelve loaves were baked weekly for the Sabbath and were displayed on the table for seven days. Sifted eleven times, the flour (called the *solet*) produced the finest wheat loaves which, according to Josephus, were unleavened. They were shaped with each end turned upwards to resemble the Ark of the Covenant. Five of the loaves were eaten by the high priest, and the remaining seven were given to the priests to eat while standing within the inner court — where only kings could sit.

The Bread of the Presence provided food for the priests and would appear to reflect the food produced in the garden for Adam's sustenance. Loaves were baked on Friday for the Sabbath ceremony that included removing the old loaves, dividing them among the priests, and replacing the old loaves with new. "On the festivals, the table would be raised aloft

[…] and displayed to the pilgrims. The priests would call out: 'Behold how precious you are to G-d! The bread was removed as required, but though seven days have passed, they are still hot as if freshly baked'" (BT *Menachot* 29a).

> The fact that the table is described as pure teaches that the priests like to display the showbread to the Festival pilgrims, and they say to them: So how beloved you are before the Omnipresent, as the bread is hot at its removal on Shabbat, after a week on the table as it was at its arrangement…at the same time it is clear that the miracle of the showbread was a miracle performed outside the sanctuary, as it was visible to all.
>
> (BT *Yoma* 21A)

The table was constructed to include molds specially designed to hold the twelve loaves. The priests arranged the bread on the table just as they arranged the pieces of meat on the altar of burnt offering. "You prepare [arrange] a table before me in the presence of my enemies" (Ps. 23.5). The Hebrew word for table is *shulcan* from the root *shalach* — meaning to "send out" or "send forth." The *Shiloach*, Pool of Siloam, comes from the same root. An apostle or emissary who is "sent out" is called a *shliach*. Both Moses and *Yeshua* were described as "sent ones." A picture emerges of the twelve set apart loaves, filled with the Presence of G-d, being sent forth from the "altar" to bring life to the people. At the time of *Yeshua*, this was fulfilled in the ministry of his twelve *talmadim* (disciples).

After King Saul had moved the Tabernacle to *Nov*, David and his men approached the High Priest *Ahimelech* (my brother is king) requesting food. "Now, therefore, what have you on hand? Give me *five* loaves of bread in my hand, or whatever can be found" (1 Sam. 21.3). With no "common bread" available, the twelve loaves of the Presence were offered to David once it was confirmed the men had "guarded themselves against women." In the Temple, priests who served could not marry women who were defiled, which included prostitutes or women who were divorced from their husbands. It is likely that David eating the bread was a picture of Adam's original status in the garden as both priest and king. It would be *the* Messiah, of the royal line of David, who would ultimately restore that role.

Like David and his men, *Yeshua's* disciples became hungry. They combed the fields plucking and eating heads of grain on the *Shabbat*. The chief priests and ruling elites declared this was a violation. *Yeshua* responded this way:

> Haven't you read what David did when he became hungry, and those with him? How he entered the house of G-d, and they ate the showbread, which was not permitted for him to eat, nor those with him, but only for the *kohanim* (priests)? Or haven't you read in the Torah that on *Shabbat* the *kohanim* in the Temple break *Shabbat* and yet are innocent? But I tell you that something greater than the Temple is here...the Son of Man is Lord of *Shabbat*.
>
> (MATTHEW 12.3–6,8)

Each loaf was baked with two *omers* (portions) of wheat — like the double portion of manna the children of Israel collected on the sixth day (in the wilderness camp) that provided "leftovers" for the Sabbath. When *Yeshua* fed the five thousand, he distributed the loaves of barley bread. Ordering the crowd to recline on the grass, he took the *five* loaves and the two fish; looking up to heaven, he offered the *brachah* (blessing). Once they ate and were satisfied, the disciples collected twelve baskets of "leftover" pieces.

A midrash on Ruth (2.14) explains, "And she ate in this world, and she was sufficed in the Days of Messiah, and she had leftover in the World to Come" (BT *Shabbat* 113b). As the great grandmother of King David, Ruth confirmed the eternal destiny of his House. *Yeshua* (Son of David) was declaring himself to be king and high priest in bringing the Bread of the Presence, the eternal food, out from the Holy Place to feed the people. "Days of Messiah" represented the intersection between this world and the world to come — in the garden. In the Messianic period, G-d will reveal the path to Eden for Israel (BT *Ta'an* 10a). *Yeshua* fed the crowd from a never-ending supply of bread. It was a reminder that the loaves were called the "continual bread." *Yeshua*, in whom G-d placed His Presence, provided the people with both physical and spiritual nourishment.

Yeshua is the living bread that came down from Heaven. He is *the* new creation — a Temple raised up filled with G-d's Presence. Eating "leftover" manna on the seventh day (Ex. 16.29) provides eternal sustenance for those who are a Kingdom of priests. "The bread of G-d is that which [or he who] comes down from heaven and gives life to the creation (*kosmos*), is not Passover imagery: it is Day of Atonement imagery, when the bread/flesh of the great high priest gives new life to the world" (Barker 2014: 255). The bread is the *basar* (flesh) or good news — the word (seed) that became flesh and "tabernacled" among us (Jn. 1.14). *Yeshua* the Messiah, the sent one, the living bread filled with the Presence of G-d, provides everlasting sustenance to his covenant people.

At the entrance to the Holy of Holies stood the Altar of Incense. Like the Ark of the Covenant, it was made from acacia wood and overlaid with pure gold. Its square top had a golden horn in each of the four corners. The altar was carried by poles which were inserted into the golden rings fastened to the sides. On *Yom Kippur* (Day of Atonement), the high priest sprinkled blood over the ark, against the curtains, and on the horns of the Altar of Incense which corresponded to the tablets inside the Ark.

The high priest (or an associate) burned incense every morning and evening on the golden altar. Incense was produced from a combination of crushed seeds, resins, bark, and gums to create a sweet aroma that permeated the Temple. On *Yom Kippur*, incense was also added to the shovelful of hot coals placed between the poles of the Ark of the Covenant. Philo compared the four incense spices (Ex. 30.34) to "a symbol of the elements [air, water, fire, and earth] out of which the whole world was brought to completion" (*Who is the Heir?* 197). Fresh coals from fig wood burning on the great altar were carried in a golden bowl and arranged on the incense altar. As the daily incense was being offered, those in the Temple precincts stood by, motionless at first, then began to pray (Luke 1.8–10, Rev. 8.1). "Hear my voice when I call to You. May my prayer be set before you like incense" (Ps. 141.2). The smoke rising from the incense altar is a reminder of G-d cutting an Eternal Covenant with Abraham as the burning torch and smoking furnace passed through the animal parts (Gen. 15).

There is some confusion surrounding the location of the Altar of Incense based on a passage in Hebrews. "Beyond the second curtain was a dwelling called the Holy of Holies. It held a golden Altar of Incense and the Ark of the Covenant, completely covered with gold" (Heb. 9.3,4). A similar description appears in the book of Revelation when the Lamb opens the seventh seal. "Another angel stood at the altar holding much incense to offer up along with the prayers of all the *kedoshim* (saints) upon the golden altar before the throne" (Rev. 8.3,4). "The sixth angel trumpeted, and I heard a single voice from the four horns of the golden altar before G-d" (9.13). Here, too, the Altar of Incense is directly before the throne. It appears the curtain separating the Holy of Holies from the Holy Place has been removed. This may suggest the renewing of the Eternal Covenant is now complete: Heaven and Earth are one. "Then I saw a new heaven and a new earth; for the first heaven and the first earth had passed away and the sea was no more" (21.1).

The *menorah* resembled a stylized tree with three pairs of outstretched branches. It was *the* symbol of the Tree of Life in the garden; its central stalk was the embodiment of the divine king. Four cups shaped like almond flowers with buds and blossoms were prominently displayed on its trunk. "Moses entered the *Ohel Edut* (tent of witness) and behold Aaron's rod had sprouted, blossomed, and produced almonds" (Num. 17.8). Perhaps Aaron's staff budding with almonds (and placed inside the ark) was originally from the Tree of Life.

The *Apocalypse of Moses* describes the chariot throne resting at the Tree of Life. "Rest" was an idiom for being seated on the throne. In the *Letter of Barnabas* (8.5), "*Yeshua's* royal kingdom was founded on a tree."

> I saw Paradise, and in the midst, the Tree of Life, at the place where the Lord takes his rest when he goes [up] to Paradise...that tree is indescribable for pleasantness and fragrance, and more beautiful than any created thing. Its appearance is gold and crimson and with the form of fire.
>
> (2 ENOCH 8.3, 4)

Aaron, the High Priest, trimmed the wicks of the *menorah* in the Tabernacle. "He [was] to arrange the lamps in order on the pure gold *menorah* before *Adonai* continually" (Lev. 24.4). The golden *menorah* in the sanctuary resembled a tree with branches, flowers, and bowls shaped like almond blossoms (Ex. 25:31–33). During the Second Temple period, five lamps were trimmed in the morning and two in the afternoon. Ten *menorot* stood in the Holy Place in the First Temple: "The lampstands of pure gold, five on the right side and five on the left in front of the inner sanctuary" (1 Kings 7.49). The priests serving in the Holy Place must have felt as though they were walking with the Presence of G-d in a brightly lit forest — like Adam in the garden.

The number five is consistently linked to the Tabernacle: its measurements were all divisible by five. In the book of Daniel (2.3–46), four Gentile kingdoms are characterized as a man-made statue — an enormous, dazzling image that was struck by a stone cut from a mountain not made by human hands. (Mountains were synonymous with temples.) It had become great and filled the whole earth. The fifth kingdom crushed the previous four along with their rulers. "Now in the days of those kings, the G-d of heaven will set up a kingdom that will never be destroyed…it will crush and bring to end all these kingdoms. But it will endure forever" (44,45).

Yeshua was *the* mountain/Temple that reunited Heaven and Earth. His resurrected body forged the new creation. Filled with G-d's Presence, He revealed to His *talmadim* (disciples) how the Garden/Kingdom should function. The service of the Bread of the Presence meant He is the continual bread that gives wisdom. The service at the Altar of Incense portrayed Him as a fragrant cloud that rises up so His priests can communicate daily with G-d. The *menorah* shows He is the true light that shines in the darkness. The Holy Place, once only visible to the Temple *kohanim* or the pilgrims on feast days, was now visible to those who had become a "Kingdom of priests" and a "royal priesthood." In time, when the Kingdom is fully restored and Heaven and Earth become one, Messiah's Kingdom priests will pass through the final curtain and come "face to face" with G-d (Rev. 21,22).

✡   ✡   ✡

Researching the structure of the Temple is essential to understanding how the Kingdom operates. If we are to be a "Kingdom of priests," cultivating and mediating on behalf of the world, then learning the purpose and function of the services and ceremonies is critical. The following fictional account, based on information from the *Mishnah*, describes how the priests performed the daily service of the *menorah* inside the Holy Place.

Yonah tossed and turned throughout the night. He could hardly contain his excitement! His mind raced in preparation for the morning's activities. *Yonah* was desperate for sleep, but so many details flooded his thoughts. He could leave nothing to chance! A tinge of apprehension clouded his excitement: *What if I forget parts of the service? What if I fail to execute my assigned task properly? What if the wrong blessing is uttered? What if…?* Yonah finally drifted off to sleep.

It was the young priest's first week to serve in the Temple. Descended from the course of *Yeshua*, the ninth *mishmar* (division or course), *Yonah* had carefully trained for the better part of a year. Upon arriving at the Temple, he scurried past the throngs of people to make his way up to the *azarah* (inner courtyard) where he stood transfixed by the towering gate complexes and the sheer immensity of the Temple building itself. The dizzying array of sights and sounds overwhelmed his senses — especially the pungent smell of the burnt offerings wafting through the Temple precincts. *Yonah* had been to the Temple for the pilgrimage festivals many times as a young boy, but he had never stood inside the *azarah*. Today was different. Today, he was a young man officially serving in the royal priesthood. *Yonah's* priestly course replaced the previous week's division. The head of the course divided *Yonah's* mishmar into six "families" or "clans" called the *Batai Av* (Houses of the Fathers). Each day of the week, one family would perform that day's services. On *Shabbat*, the entire team served together. *Yonah's* clan, *Harim*, had been chosen to serve on the first day of the week: *Yom Rishon* or Sunday.

Yonah felt himself being shaken awake. His colleague *Sha'ul* whispered, "*Yonah*, wake up." It was pitch dark as he struggled to open his eyes. The first lottery of the day would start soon in the *Beit HaMoked* (House of the Hearth). This lottery included preparing the *kior* (laver) for the ritual hand and foot washing and removing the previous day's ashes from the Great Altar. If he were to participate in this lottery, *Yonah* would need to immerse and then dress in his priestly garments before the first light of day appeared.

The *Beit HaMoked* was an immense four-chambered,

dome-covered building in the northwest corner of the *azarah*. Temple guards were stationed there, and it served as a dormitory for the weekly division of *kohanim* (priests) who conducted the daily services. One chamber contained stone-slabbed steps that jutted out from the inner walls to form platforms that were narrower on the top level and wider on the bottom. These compact "cubbies" were the sleeping quarters for the priests. From inside his small cubicle on the lower level of the *Beit HaMoked*, *Yonah* observed a Temple official grabbing hold of a silver hoop fastened to a small trap door embedded in the marble floor of the building.

As the elder slowly raised the marble section of flooring, *Yonah* caught sight of a set of keys dangling from a chain attached to the inside of the trap door. That was his cue. *Yonah*, barefoot, hurried down the cold, stone steps to the immersion bath — required for entry into the *azarah*. Every *kohen* (priest) who desired to perform the services rose early to purify himself in the "living waters" of the *mikvah* (immersion bath). *Yonah* dried off and warmed his cold feet by the fire for which *HaMoked* (hearth) was named. He heard loud knocking coming from upstairs followed by a booming voice, "Whoever has by now immersed himself should come and draw lots to determine who picks up the ashes from the altar." *Yonah* hurried back upstairs to await the arrival of the lottery supervisor. He heard the *g'vinay* (Temple announcer) cry out, "Rise up! Priests arise and begin your duties! Levites, to your platform! Israelites, man your stations!"

Within the main gate of the *Beit HaMoked* was another gate that opened onto the *azarah*. The elder who had opened the trap door handed the keys to an official who then unlocked the small gate. Another priest carried a torch to light the way for the *kohanim* (priests) as they followed behind. The *kohanim* split into two units to inspect the Temple's ninety-three vessels for any impurities. *Yonah* was part of the first group. He entered the *azarah* heading east following the portico which ran along the inner wall. The second group turned right to head west. They found that none of the vessels had been disturbed during the night. The two groups eventually met at the Chamber of the *Havitim* where the pancake makers and bread offerors kneaded and baked the daily meal offerings. *Yonah's* unit arrived first — their route being slightly shorter. Once both groups reached the chamber, all the *kohanim* loudly proclaimed, "Peace! Everything is at peace!"

The second lottery took place in the Chamber of Hewn Stone — home to the Great Sanhedrin. This lottery included the *Tamid* (daily offering), the removing of excess ash from the golden incense altar, and the servicing of the *menorah* (lampstand): cleaning out the old wicks and ash from the *menorah's* cups and adding fresh oil. *Yonah* held his breath. He had prayed many times for the honor of attending the golden, seven-branched *menorah*.

Thirteen different priestly assignments were also a part of this second lottery. The *kohanim* formed a large circle. A Temple official stepped into the center. When asked, *Yonah* removed his turban and handed it to the official, meaning he was the starting point for the counting. The official chose a number larger than those *kohanim* present, and each priest held out either one or two fingers. The overseer began to count fingers, starting with *Yonah*, round and round, "*echad, shnayim, shlosha…*" (one, two, three…), until the first priest was chosen. The second priest, adjacent to the first, was charged with receiving the blood in the sacrificial vessel. The third would remove the ashes from the incense altar; *Sh'aul* was picked for that duty. *Yonah*, fourth in line, was chosen to service the golden *menorah*. Though he held his emotions in check, he secretly reveled in this remarkable opportunity.

As *Yonah* exited the Chamber of Hewn Stone, he spotted a priest ascending the "pinnacle" located atop the Spark Gate. This priest, called the "watchman," was responsible for monitoring the sun's ascent from the eastern horizon. *Yonah* felt a chill in the air. Overnight, a dense fog had filled the valleys surrounding Jerusalem and had silently crept up the sides of Mount Moriah. The sun's first rays pierced the moisture-laden air and revealed a rainbow-colored hue crossing the valley. It reminded *Yonah* of "the sign" given to Noah after the flood — the bow which confirmed G-d's eternal covenant with His creation. Billowing clouds began to break apart, and light came streaming forth from the hills of Hebron. The column of dew evaporated as the watchman shouted from the pinnacle, "*Barchai!*" The priests below waited for his second announcement, "The entire eastern horizon is illuminated!" *Yonah* heard his colleague call up, "Does the glow extend all the way to Hebron?" "Yes!" the watchman replied.

Yonah remembered his father speaking of one born "King of the Jews" who had ascended the pinnacle of the Royal Stoa. There the devil had enticed him saying, "If you are the Son of G-d, jump off!" *Yonah* knew it was a long way down.

A Temple official ascended the twelve steps before the sanctuary. He was tasked with opening the northern wicket of the sanctuary's Great Gate. The southern wicket was never opened — for no man ever passed through it. Tradition held that only the *Nasi* (prince) with the key of David could enter that gate and leave the same way. The prophet Ezekiel said, "This gate shall be shut; it shall not be opened because His Presence has gone through it."

Together, *Yonah* and *Sha'ul* mounted the Temple steps carrying four items between them: a golden basket for the incense altar's ashes, a golden jug shaped like an over-sized wine goblet to hold the residue from the menorah, and two keys. After passing through the Great Gate, the pair followed the inner wall of the sanctuary until they came upon a gold-plated door that was locked. The outer lock opened immediately; the inside lock proved more difficult. Once through, they entered a narrow passageway which led to another chamber at the northeast corner of the Temple. By this time, *Yonah* was thoroughly disoriented and was grateful for *Sha'ul* who was familiar with the twists and turns of the Temple's inner corridors.

Sha'ul entered the Holy Place first. He set down his golden basket in front of the golden Altar of Incense and began to remove the ash with his bare hands — placing it in the container. He used a small brush to sweep up the remaining ash. His task complete, *Sha'ul* left the basket on the floor and departed the sanctuary. That was *Yonah's* cue. He inhaled deeply, swallowed hard, and with great solemnity approached the golden *menorah*. It stood majestically on the southern side of the Holy Place in an east-west orientation perpendicular to the *parokhet* (curtain). Six golden branches proudly extended diagonally upward from a central shaft. The three branches on the west and the three on the east both faced the middle lamp — their wicks pointing upward.

Yonah began cleaning out the five lamps, called "improving the five flames" or "dressing the candles." He ascended the three marble steps to the platform in front of the *menorah* which allowed him to perform the service at eye level. He carefully removed the excess oil and cleaned out the ash and the wicks — putting them into the golden pitcher. *Yonah* replenished the five with freshly pressed, pure olive oil: one-half lug. The *Ner Ma'arvi*, the western lamp on the middle shaft, was still burning. It was kindled each evening from the fire of the Great Altar. A perpetual flame, it testified that the *shekinah*, the divine Presence, was *the* light. It has been said that up to the death of the High Priest, *Shimon* the *Tzaddik* (at the time of Alexander the Great), the western flame constantly burned without the need of additional oil. It was considered a miracle; the flame showed the Divine Presence dwelled "in the midst" of Israel. *Yonah* dressed the last remaining lamp, took up his golden pitcher, and joined with *Sha'ul* to dump the refuse on the floor by the Great Altar.

Yonah reflected on the ancient meaning of the *menorah*: Wisdom personified as a Tree of Life, the Light of the World, and a golden tree that symbolized the great lights in the heavens. *Yonah* knew the *menorah* occupied *the* most central role of all the sacred vessels. It was a symbol of light — the light of the Divine Presence — and it represented the Tree of Life in the garden: a verdant tree of indescribable beauty whose blossoms dripped with a celestial fragrance, branches glowed vermillion, and fire-like leaves hid ambrosial fruit. The central shaft of the *menorah* represented the Davidic king who gave life to the entire world from the place where Heaven and Earth converged: The Temple. The *menorah* symbolized *the* Divine Presence as a Tree of Light and a Tree of Fire with light radiating from the garden to the whole world. It stood as an echo of the *Brit Esh*, the Covenant of Fire, seen by Moses as he stood on holy ground and watched a bush that burned but was not consumed. Abraham saw the same Divine fire embodied in the burning torch and the smoking furnace as they passed between the animal halves.

The sound of trumpet blasts pierced *Yonah's* reverie. He turned aside to see the men of Israel prostrating themselves — stretched out on the cold pavement between the porch and the altar. The *kohanim* positioned themselves on the twelve steps just above the men. Slowly, they raised their hands above their heads and spoke The NAME as they chanted the soulful, melodious tones of the Aaronic benediction, "*Y'varechah Adonai, v'yish mirechah, yair Adonai, panev elichah, vichu necha.*" (The Lord bless you and keep you, the Lord make His face to shine upon you.) With that, a heavenly blessing fell like dew upon the people, and they were revived.

Trees in the Sacred Center

At the place where creation was birthed, two trees sprouted from moistened clods of earth. Swollen buds blossomed producing bright green leaves with luscious fruit. They grew until their canopies towered over the garden sanctuary; thick branches reached up to the heavens, and their roots pressed deep into the soil. In the sacred center, at the crossroads of the universe, the trees stretched out their limbs towards Earth's four corners. They served as pillars that supported both the heavens above and the earth below and embodied the unity of Heaven and Earth. Along the banks of Eden's river, other trees bore fruit that yielded food each month. Filled with the seeds of the Spirit, the fruit produced love, joy, peace, patience, goodness, gentleness, kindness, faithfulness, and self-control to provide healing and restoration to the nations.

✡ ✡ ✡

These arboreal elements are perhaps *the* most recognizable symbols in the Bible (Some scholars have suggested there was only one tree). Over the centuries, many theories for their meaning have been proposed. In explaining the choice of a tree to represent the concepts of life, Earth, and Heaven in ancient cultures, Terje Stordalen wrote, "Every green tree would symbolize life, and a large tree — rooted in deep soil and stretching towards the sky — potentially makes a cosmic symbol." Lundquist explains that the Temple, as a cosmic tree, also "originates in the underworld, stands on the earth as a 'meeting place,' and yet towers [architecturally] into the heavens and gives access to the heavens through its ritual" (2002: 675).

In the ANE, a great tree stood at the world's center and was referred to as a tree of life. The tree symbolized divine order and represented the kings. "Its roots [were] fed by the great subterranean ocean and its top [merged] with the clouds and thus [bound] together the heavens, the earth, and the netherworld" (Walton 2006: 75–76). Michael Fishbane in his article, "The Symbolism of the Sacred Center" describes the garden as the *axis mundi* and that from it radiated primal streams to the four quarters of the earth. "It was and is the navel, or omphalos, and the Tree of Life stands at the center of this center." Regarded as the abode for the indwelling deity, the sacred tree in the ANE was thought to draw on the divine through its roots and so it was always associated with water — such as the Gihon Spring. The wise one, who delights in the Torah of G-d, is compared to a tree transplanted in channels of water, producing fruit in season, sprouting leaves that never wither, and becoming successful in all that he does (Ps. 1.2,3).

Trees symbolized divinity. They were regarded as oracles, vehicles of knowledge and wisdom, through which the divine communicated (George and George 2014: 144). Trees were often associated with a goddess such as Isis, Nut, Asherah, or Ishtar — as well as the dying or rising god who represented the cycle of the seasons (148). The *menorah* (fem. noun) was a stylized tree that functioned in much the same way. Some suggest the Tree of Life was an almond tree with the *menorah* as its symbol. According to one legend, the prophet Zechariah received a vision of a man "standing among the trees of the Tabernacle" based on the paneling, the pillars, and the *menorot* of the main hall. "In the midst of the *menorot*, I saw One like a Son of Man, clothed in a robe down to His feet, with a golden belt wrapped around his chest" (Rev. 1.13) could refer to the king-priest (Solomon) in the House of the Forest of Lebanon (see below) in the First Temple and Adam in the garden.

Rashi said the Tree of Knowledge was a fig tree; the Ark of the Covenant was its symbol. "The Tree of Knowledge of Good and Evil represented the *axis mundi* and as such was the link for humans to access divinity" (George and George 2014: 120). The two great pillars leading into the First Temple were adorned with lilies and were decorated as two large trees covered with two-hundred pomegranates each (1 Kings 7:19–20). Over time, the sacred tree evolved into many other forms: columns, pillars, standing stones, towers, altars, vines, stalks, ladders, stairways, scepters, and ultimately the cross itself. Modern architecture captures a similar theme with its capitol buildings, palaces, monuments, skyscrapers, minarets, spires, and steeples.

The garden sanctuary, located to the east of Eden, was filled with countless varieties of trees — reminiscent of kings' gardens in the ANE. Standing on the steps at the entrance to this stylized Temple forest, a worshipper might well be inspired by the representations of trees in gemstones, coral, seashells, and shining bronze and copper (SD Dalley). The Holy Place in the First Temple was framed with beams from cedar trees then paneled with carved cedarwood and overlaid with gold. "The righteous man flourishes like a date palm, grows tall as a cedar in Lebanon, is planted in the house of the Lord, where they flourish in the courts of our G-d" (Ps. 92–13–14). Cedars of Lebanon, prized wood for building palaces and temples in the ANE, were remarkably long-lived (over 1000 years). One reason a new king began military campaigns in the region was to take control over the cedar forests in Lebanon (the only major stand of cedars) for use in constructing his palace and temple (Matthews 2002: 20). Cedars in the Bible symbolized strength, endurance, wealth, and longevity for the ruling king.

I will plant in the wilderness the cedar and the acacia tree, the myrtle and the olive tree. I will set in the desert the cypress tree and the pine together with the box tree — so they may see and know, consider and understand together, that the hand of *Adonai* has done this, the Holy One of Israel has created it.

(ISAIAH 41.19)

Cedars of Lebanon used to construct Solomon's palace also provided the pillars for the House of the Forest of Lebanon. Adjacent to his royal complex, King Solomon built a stone-walled, rectangular shaped forest house for storing armor. During the reign of his son Rehoboam, Shishak (King of Egypt), carried off the armor from the forest chamber.

King Rehoboam later replaced the copper shields (1 Kings 14.25–28; 2 Chron. 12.9–11). "He will expose Judah's defense, and in that day, you will look for the armor in the Forest House" (Is. 22.8). The armory was designed with four rows (three rows according to the Septuagint) of cedar pillars, cedar beams laid out over the forty-five pillars, and panels of cedar above the beams (1 Kings 7.2–4). The hall contained five hundred large and small shields of beaten gold (2 Chron. 9.15–16). Some have suggested live cedars were brought in to give the hall its forest smell. "Just as the forest is fruitful and multiplies, even so the sanctuary, everything that was in it was fruitful and multiplied (Patai 1967: 90). It has been suggested that the House of the Forest of Lebanon followed the tripartite layout of the Temple, in that the Hall of the Pillars corresponded to the porch, the forest chamber to the Holy Place (the garden), and the Hall of Judgment to the Holy of Holies (Eden).

A description, "window opposite window in three tiers," has led some scholars to speculate that Solomon created an optical illusion to give his visitors the sense of entering a forest rather than a pillared hall. To produce this effect, Solomon may have included a few dozen live trees. "It was the use of facing mirrors at both ends of each one of the 'see through passages' that gave the visitor the illusion of being in an infinite forest—the trees reflected endlessly in the opposing mirrors" (Hareuveni 1984: 103).

✡   ✡   ✡

The kings of Judah, as well as the kings of Israel, were often compared to the great cedar trees for their pride and arrogance. Ezekiel referred to Jehoiakim's evil son as the very "top" of the cedar. Jeremiah also railed against King Jehoiakim for his extravagant projects built on the backs of the people. "I will build myself a big house with spacious rooms and cut out my windows for it, and panel it with cedar and paint it with vermilion! *Adonai* responded, 'Did you become king just to be striving with cedar?'" (Jer. 22.13–17).

Pharaoh and the king of Assyria were also compared to cedars — ones that were cut down for their arrogance.

> Son of man, say to Pharaoh King of Egypt and to his multitude, who is like you in your greatness? Behold, Assyria was a cedar in Lebanon, with beautiful branches shadowing the forest, of lofty height. Its top was in leafy branches. Water nourished it, the deep made it tall, with its rivers going around its planting as it sent out its watercourses to all the trees of the field. Therefore, its height was loftier than all the trees of the field…all great nations lived under its shade.
>
> (EZEKIEL 31.1–8)

> I will take from a sprig from the top of the lofty cedar and will plant it. I will crop off a tender twig from the topmost of its young shoots and I will plant it on a tall and prominent mountain. I will plant it on Israel's high mountain. It will bring forth branches, bear fruit and be a magnificent cedar. Birds of every kind will nest under it — they will nest in the shade of its branches. Then all the trees of the field will know that I, *Adonai*, have brought down the high tree, exalted the lowly tree, dried up the green tree, and made the dry tree flourish.
>
> (EZEKIEL 17.22–24)

Symbolically, trees represented priests and kings whose vocation meant cultivating the garden. As righteous image-bearers, these trees were to bear fruit and create shade (sovereignty) for the world to enjoy." Like an apple tree among the trees of the forest, so is my lover among the sons. In his shadow, I delighted to sit, and his fruit was sweet to my taste" (Song of Songs 2.3). In the Dead Sea Scrolls, the Qumran community is compared to an Edenic tree:

Its shoot growing into the branches of the eternal planting and its shade spreading all over the earth, its top reaching to Heaven, the rivers of Eden watering it so it becomes a forest that spreads over the world without end, a well spring of light and brilliant flames.

(1QH 6.12–19)

"The new Eden's tree will grow its branches over the entire globe and its shade will spread until the earth is under a massive arboreal like tabernacle" (Beale 2004: 156–158). "All the earth will become Eden: after all sin has been extinguished from the earth" (157n). The commission to be fruitful and multiply and fill the earth began in the garden sanctuary. John describes the "new creation" in Revelation as a giant Edenic sanctuary (Rev. 21).

My heart was pruned and its flower appeared...and it produced fruits for the Lord. And from above he gave me immortal rest; and I became like the land which blossoms and rejoices in its fruits...and he took me to Paradise...I contemplated blooming and fruit bearing trees...their branches flourishing and their fruits shining. And who grow in the growth of your trees, and have passed from darkness into light.

(ODES OF SOLOMON 11–12)

When the disciples arrived in Bethsaida, the townspeople brought a blind man to *Yeshua*. "He took the man by the hand and led him outside the village. After spitting on the man's eyes and laying his hands on him, *Yeshua* asked, 'Do you see anything?' The blind man looked up and said, 'I see men! They look like trees walking about.' *Yeshua* put his hands on the man's eyes again. The man looked intently, his sight was restored, and he began to see everything clearly" (Mk. 8.22–25). The details surrounding this miracle seem strange, but saliva was considered a valid treatment for blindness due to its healing properties. Also, "[there] is a tradition that the spittle of the firstborn of a father is healing" (BT *Baba Batra* 126b).

What did the man see? Trees walking! He saw a vision of the garden sanctuary filled with trees. It was the Holy Place in the Temple where priests, resembling "living, breathing trees," served. In the natural realm, entry was forbidden to everyone except the Levitical priesthood and especially forbidden to those with a defect such as blindness. The blind man's eyes were opened, and yet he hadn't died. His eyes were opened, and he wasn't naked or afraid. His eyes were opened, and he had no need to hide "in the midst" of the trees away from the Presence of G-d. He had come "face to face" with *Yeshua*, the One who established the Kingdom of Heaven on Earth, and he was welcomed with love and compassion.

It's not surprising, therefore, that the Kingdom/Temple on Earth was inaugurated from a tree. Peter wrote, "They put him to death by hanging him on a tree, but G-d raised him up on the third day and caused him to be visible — not to all people, but to us, witnesses who were chosen beforehand by G-d" (Acts 39–41a). These witnesses then shared a covenant meal with Messiah which confirmed they were a new creation: "We ate and drank with him after he rose from the dead. And he commanded us to proclaim to the people and to testify that he is the One ordained by G-d as judge of the living and the dead…that everyone who puts his trust in him receives forgiveness of sins through his name" (41b).

Why Trees?

In the ANE, an image of the deity was placed inside the local temple. The king stood in for the god as his living representative on earth. From the throne, the king guaranteed stability in the political and social realm on behalf of the god. If the king was absent, perhaps fighting a war abroad, then an idol cut from a tree, chiseled from stone, or fire-gilded with precious metals was placed in the temple to represent the king, but with the face of the god. This likely explains the incident of the golden calf in which Aaron made a molten calf and fashioned it with a chiseling tool. The people complained that they did not know what had become of their "king" Moses. "Now when the people saw that Moses delayed in coming down the mountain (a temple), they gathered around Aaron and said to him, 'Get up, make us gods who will go before us'" (Ex. 32.1).

In Israel, G-d's representative, the king, did not capture His physical features, but, rather, "those aspects of the king's appearance that had been molded by the gods and that resembled the gods, such that ruler's features convey qualities of ideal, divinely-sanctioned rulership, not just personhood" (Walton 2009: 21). G-d placed (rested) His image-bearing king in the garden as the functional ideal. As the human/king representative of G-d's Presence, Adam was to expand the Kingdom outward, maintain order and stability through acts of priestly service, and preserve the covenant unity between Heaven and Earth.

A parable about trees from the book of Judges (9) echoes this theme. After Gideon's successful attack on the Midianites, the elders of Israel offered him the rulership of Israel. Gideon responded, "I will not rule over you, nor shall my son rule over you; the Lord shall rule over you" (Judges 8:21–23 NASB). The responsibility to govern Israel was then passed down to Gideon's seventy sons. *Avimelech* (my father is king), the illegitimate son, declared himself king after slaughtering all seventy sons. Only Jotham, the youngest, escaped.

Although the identity of the trees in Judges (9) was likely tied to specific judges of that period, there is a deeper significance related to Israel. The olive tree represented King David, the fig tree King Saul, and the vine King Solomon. Each ruled forty years over Israel — a number associated with the natural world. By contrast, the bramble or thorn bush, which was

Avimelech, the enemy within, represented the ruling elites of the Temple who continually oppressed the people. They were ultimately responsible for the nation's exile and the land being devoured by Israel's enemies.

✡   ✡   ✡

The sages connected garden to the Temple because it was built with cedar trees from Lebanon. "And when the gentiles entered the Sanctuary the golden tree withered, and the blossoms of Lebanon withered" (Nah. 1.4). "And the Holy One, blessed be He, will restore the miraculous trees to Israel in the future. It shall blossom abundantly, it shall also rejoice and shout, the glory of Lebanon will be given to it" (BT *Yoma* 21b).

Trimming the *menorah*, presenting the bread, and attending the incense altar were daily duties of the priests. They were surrounded by the majesty, splendor, and holiness of the Temple environment as they performed the services. By the Second Temple period, however, some of the Sadducean chief priests failed to appreciate the glorious setting in which they served — likely forgetting even the purpose of their heavenly vocation. *Yeshua* criticized and denounced these ruling authorities for turning the sacred space into their personal fiefdom from which to control the people. He criticized the Temple leadership, often in a cryptic manner, for failing to bring justice and mercy to the nation and for causing the sanctuary to become defiled. *Yeshua* accused them of being blind guides leading blind sheep and erecting obstacles that prevented the poor, the downtrodden, and the afflicted from "drawing near" to the Kingdom. Some of the chief priests continually promoted themselves among men by taking the place of honor at feasts and by hoarding the best seats in the synagogue (Matt. 23) while neglecting those truly in need.

G-d planted His garden and filled it with fruit-bearing trees to represent human beings. He desired that His "righteous" image-bearers flourish like date palms and cedars and yield fruit in old age as they maintained G-d's justice in the world. "Blessed is the one who trusts in *Adonai*, whose confidence is in *Adonai*. For he will be like a tree planted by the waters, spreading out roots by a stream" (Jer. 17.7,8). With *Yeshua's* launch of the Kingdom, the eyes of the blind were opened, the deaf could hear, and those brought low were raised up. He consoled those mourning in Zion with the oil of joy and with the garment of praise, so they were called "trees of righteousness" and the planting of the Lord (Is. 61.3).

CHAPTER THREE

THE FIELD

You visit the earth and water it, You greatly enrich it;
The river of G-d is full of water;
You provide their grain, for so You have prepared it
You water its ridges abundantly, You settle its furrows;
You make it soft with showers,
You bless its growth.
(Psalm 65.9)

The Bride

In the beginning, G-d cut a covenant with Heaven and Earth
and bound them together in marriage. The Heavens represented the bridegroom and the Earth the bride. Their union
formed G-d's Cosmic House, and from the womb of the earth
(ancient cultures believed the womb equaled a sanctuary) the

seed of creation sprouted. "He [the angel] said to me, even so have I given the womb of the Earth to those who from time to time are sown in it" (2 Esdras 5.48). The House was *kallah* (meaning complete or a bride who completes her husband) along with its entire array (Gen. 2.1). On the Seventh Day, the sanctified House overflowed with G-d's Presence and produced fruit. "These are the *toldot* (genealogy: from the root *yalad* meaning to bring forth or bear children) of the heavens and the earth when they were created" (Gen. 2.4).

G-d formed the man into the image of a small, ordered world — a miniature cosmos. The man became a living being, male and female, in G-d's image. G-d "took" a woman from the man's *tsel* (shade or image) and *banah* (built) her into His great House. The man and his wife expressed fidelity to G-d by cultivating His garden sanctuary and by extending His glory to Earth's four corners. On Earth, the woman was the visible representation of the heavenly Tabernacle: "Jerusalem above that is free — who is our mother" (Gal. 4.26). Called Jerusalem as well as *bat Tziyon*, the virgin daughter of Zion, the woman typified G-d's House. "Come I will show you the bride, the wife of the Lamb. Then he carried me away in the *Ruach* (spirit) to a great and high mountain and he showed me the holy city, Jerusalem [the bride] coming down out of Heaven from G-d, having the glory of G-d — her radiance was like a most precious stone, like a jasper, and sparkling like crystal" (Rev. 21.10,11).

Song of Songs describes G-d's bride and beloved as His garden: "a locked garden is my sister, my bride, an enclosed spring, a sealed fountain. Your shoots are an orchard of pomegranates with choice fruit...with all the trees of frankincense, myrrh, and aloes, along with all the finest spices — a garden spring, a well of living water and flowing streams from Lebanon" (4.12–15). G-d is the bridegroom who takes pleasure in His garden: "Instead you will be called, 'My Delight is in Her' and your land 'Married.' For as a young man marries a virgin, so your sons will marry you" (Is. 62.5). The sages have suggested that the Song of Songs speak of both the Holy of Holies in the Temple and the Ark of the Covenant as the couch. The ark is a traveling couch, the portable throne of G-d, resting in the midst of the people.

> Who is this — she who is coming up from the wilderness like columns of smoke, perfumed with myrrh and frankincense, with every powder of the merchant? Behold it is Solomon's traveling couch — around it sixty warriors from the warriors of Israel. King Solomon has made for himself a carriage from the trees of Lebanon. He made its posts of silver, its back of gold, its seat of purple cloth, its interior fitted out with love by the daughters of Jerusalem.
>
> (SONG OF SONGS 3.6-10)

In Song of Songs, the Temple is compared to Solomon's bride being prepared for her wedding day. She is a young virgin daughter — a beautifully decorated temple. Her cheeks are adorned with light and her neck showcases a string of luminescent beads. On her arms dangle ornaments of gold and spangles of silver (1.10, 11). The bride is black and beautiful — displaying her sun-darkened skin that resembles hides covering the tents of Kedar (1.5). Solomon wrote, "I have come into my garden, my sister, my bride" (5.1) and "You are beautiful my darling, like Tirza, lovely as Jerusalem" (6.4). His Bride was also the Tabernacle, likened to a garden sanctuary in the wilderness — the place where G-d dwelled in the midst of His people. "How lovely are your tents, O Jacob, and your dwellings, O Israel! Like valleys, they are spread out, like gardens beside a river, like aloes planted by *Adonai*, like cedars beside the waters" (Num. 24.5, 6). When the king sat on his couch, he observed beams of cedar trees and panels of cypress wood (1.17).

From Israel's seed, an immense cedar grew to become

the divine king that spread his canopy over the whole world. A sign from Heaven given to King Ahaz spoke of his son, Hezekiah — the one prophesied to cleanse, rebuild, and restore the Temple as well as continue the dynasty of King David. (Some have suggested the prophecy of the son born to the young maiden was Isaiah's firstborn. The context reveals it was Hezekiah who was born to Ahaz, King of Judah — the king who neglected the Temple and allowed it to fall into disrepair.) A virgin would conceive and bear a son and "she [would] call his name *Immanuel* — G-d with us" (Is. 7.14). (ANE women named their children except in the case of adoption). "For unto us a child is born, a son will be given to us and the government will be upon his shoulder…Of the increase of his government and *shalom*, there will be no end — on the throne of David and over his Kingdom — to establish it and uphold it through justice and righteousness from now until forevermore" (Is. 9.5, 6). The Gospels tell of an infant, born of a virgin, who was wrapped in strips of cloth and laid in a manger. The fulfilled sign is this: the daughter of Zion, G-d's Holy House, gave birth to the child who would build David's dynasty. The book of Revelation speaks of a woman clothed with the sun, with the moon under her feet and a crown of twelve stars on her head. She is pregnant — crying out in the agony of her labor (12.1,2). In the first century, this woman was *Yeshua's* mother, *Miriam* (Mary).

The destiny of the royal seed began with *Chavah*. As the first "house," she produced the line of priest-kings who would rule the Kingdom on Earth. The book of Esdras, however, suggests that each successive generation diminishes in stature, just as women age and become barren. "As the womb failed in old age, so too the creation is aging and passing the strength of youth" (Esdras 5. 51–55). When Sarah gave birth to Isaac, well past her childbearing years, the Kingdom was bearing fruit and revealing a new creation! Isaac, her son, "increased" in strength and stature, and his seed numbered the stars in the sky. Isaac is a type and shadow of *Yeshua* who kept increasing in wisdom and stature and in favor with G-d and men (Luke. 2.52). The birth of the King, Messiah, began a reversal of the decay in the natural world and a restoration of the created order.

The Bible focuses on the royal line of G-d's priest-kings and on building the dynasty of the House of David. The *toldot* of the heavens and earth that began with Adam, Son of G-d and priest-king, continued to *Noach* through Adam's son Seth, and from *Noach's* son Shem to Abraham. The seed passed from Abraham through Amram to Moses, from Boaz to King David, and ultimately to *Yeshua* the Messiah. *Yeshua* restored the monarchy after it had been cut off (with King Jehoiachin: Jer. 22.30) and rebuilt the Temple (His body), which was then filled with the Presence of G-d (Luke 3.23–38). "Behold the dwelling of G-d is among men, and He shall tabernacle among them. They shall be His people [bride] and G-d Himself shall be among them and be their G-d [groom]" (Rev. 21.3).

The Groom

G-d passed His vocation of master gardener to Adam, the human. In the sacred marriage ceremonies of the ancient world, "gardener" was the epithet given to males who became kings. Sargon 1, for example, as the son of a king and high priestess, became *the* royal gardener. He was regarded as Assyria's "tenant farmer" — meaning he was chief in serving the gods within the sacred sanctuary and in organizing the service of the priests. Consider *Yeshua's* Parable of the Tenants (Matt. 21.28–46). G-d was the original landowner, and His tenants were the religious elite who oversaw the Temple and its environs. G-d's "beloved" son (see chapter 4), the Messiah, was the legitimate successor, rightful heir, and tenant farmer who oversaw the service of the priests in the sacred space.

Adam's priestly service found fulfillment in his kinship with the *adamah*, the ground. The image-bearer was to build the dynasty through fruitful work to produce blessing and abundance and to cultivate relationships by scattering and harvesting seed. "Humanity's identity is bound to the ground by a remarkable wordplay: the *adam* and the *adamah*" (Brown 7 pillars 81). Both words are from the root, *dam*, meaning blood. Humanity is G-d's most beloved possession. Israel in Canaan paralleled Adam's vocation in the garden. Like the chief gardener, Israel promised to preserve the seed and govern the sanctuary through justice and righteousness. Transgressing the Law meant banishment from the Temple as Adam had been banished from the garden. Israel's exile allowed the sacred space to heal from the contamination of sin and the effects caused by the disease of idolatry.

Cain, the firstborn son of Adam, inherited the priest-king vocation of gardening from his father. He brought fruit from the earth to the altar as required, but a spirit of jealousy provoked him to murder his brother, Abel. G-d told him, "The voice of your brother's bloods (plural) is crying out to me from the (*adamah*) ground" (Gen. 4.10). A connection is made between ground and blood. Cain suffered a curse, and the ground split; it opened its mouth to receive Abel's blood (Gen. 4). G.K. Beale notes that whenever an earthquake is mentioned, "it denotes the chaos between [the fall of] one kingdom and [the rise of] another" (Beale and Carson 2007: 1105). Judgment came upon Cain, the next in line to be king; his "kinship" with the ground was permanently severed, and his royal seed was cut off. The ground would never again yield crops for him — a pattern that was set for all kings who violated the commandments of G-d.

Adam's vocation included preserving the seed, blessing the land, and subduing the earth under the authority of G-d. As the priestly image-bearer, Adam's stewardship also meant expanding the Kingdom through seed to cover the earth. "This goal was to be achieved by his [G-d's] human vice-regent whom he installed in the garden sanctuary to extend the garden boundaries of G-d's Presence worldwide" (Beale 2008:

137). The royal image placed in the sanctuary setting, Adam in this case, was an ancient concept found even outside Israel (129). G-d's image was revealed more and more as Adam's dynastic seed proliferated on the earth under the righteous rule of a benevolent king. In contrast, ANE kings conquered; they ravaged and pillaged land, destroyed enemies, and maintained their power through force. They ruled as autocrats and dictators; they enslaved the people by controlling the production of food, goods, and services.

The pattern is repeated with Joseph, son of Jacob, who at thirty years became Vice-regent over Egypt. He interpreted Pharaoh's dreams — highly unusual since Pharaoh, considered a god, could always interpret them himself. Joseph, raised up from the pit like Adam from the dust, subdued the earth and exercised his vocation as chief gardener. He preserved and spread the seed grain during the famine. The remainder of Jacob's sons worked as shepherds. They eventually joined Joseph in Egypt, where they settled the pasture lands of Goshen.

Appointed Egypt's Superintendent of the Granary, Joseph took charge of food production. He gathered seed during the seven years of abundance and stored the grain in supply cities "like the sand of the sea." Before the seven-year famine began, two sons were born to Joseph; the younger was Ephraim which means "G-d has made me fruitful in the land of my oppression." The older was Manasseh which means "causing to forget." Both were adopted into Israel's dynasty. Ephraim, however, received the double inheritance; his tribal territory included the capital cities and the royal families of the Northern Kingdom (also called Samaria, Israel, and Ephraim).

Wheat grain became a metaphor for righteous Israel. Israel was *kadosh* (holy) to *Adonai* — the *reisheet* (first) of the increase or produce from the threshing floor, the winepress, and the vineyard. Israel was *the* spreading seed that would preserve the world. Jacob's family re-united in Egypt during the grain famine which enabled Israel to become fruitful outside the "land." They made themselves into a mighty "house" in Egypt — producing offspring as the sand on the seashore. The family grew from seventy to more than 600,000. But, unfortunately, they never removed detestable idolatry from their midst — a pattern that would repeat.

Yeshua began his public ministry at thirty — crowned king at his immersion (Luke 3.23). Luke (4) outlines his royal lineage: from the son of Joseph, the son of Heli, back to Adam, "son of G-d" — an ANE title for the King. Instead of being elevated *to* his position from the earth or from the pit (like Adam and Joseph), *Yeshua* was raised *up* out of the water, as the *Ruach haKodesh* (Holy Spirit) came upon Him in bodily form like a dove. Out of Heaven came a voice saying, "You are my Son, whom I love — with you I am well pleased!" This is ANE language for a son receiving the royal inheritance, being officially adopted as Son of G-d, and becoming king (see chapter 4).

Yeshua increased in wisdom and stature. He expanded the Kingdom through seed, the Word of G-d, just as Joseph did. A parable explains, "[T]he one sown on the good soil, this is the one who hears the word and understands. He indeed bears fruit, yielding a hundredfold, some sixty, some thirty times what was sown" (Matt. 13.23). What is the significance of these numbers? They relate to the dynasty of the whole House of Israel. At one hundred years of age, Isaac was born to Abraham. At sixty, Jacob was born to Isaac, and at thirty, Ephraim was born to Joseph. Also at thirty, *Yeshua* was born again and elevated to rule over the Kingdom of Heaven.

After *Yeshua's* resurrection, the royal line passed on to his disciples who were a "Kingdom of priests" and a "royal priesthood" reigning on the earth (Rev. 5.10). They were the new creation image-bearers who spread the image of G-d over the earth and reflected the praises of G-d back to creation.

Their seed multiplied and increased, and it filled the world with wisdom, knowledge, and understanding. Born again in the image of Messiah, future disciples were to become a new temple filled with the Presence of G-d. They were to exercise righteousness and justice as kings; and as priests, they were to bring healing, deliverance, and freedom for captives bound by chains.

✡   ✡   ✡

The *midrashic* story continues. Adam and *Chavah* were chosen to bring order and stability to the world and to maintain creation from inside the garden. Paradise would be short-lived. After their vocational anointing, they violated the covenantal agreement that bound them to G-d's sacred space. Their disobedience caused a breach in the covenant allowing the wrath of G-d to break through; the hedge of protection they once enjoyed was removed. Exiled from the garden, they were forced to live in the field among the thistles and thorns and wild beasts. The cursed ground made it difficult to grow food and created challenges for them. The field was a hostile environment where chaos and disorder reigned and where death became a constant companion. G-d, however, in His mercy and compassion, and with divine justice, intervened on their behalf; He provided a way, through blood atonement, for them to draw near once again.

With the first part of the coronation ceremony concluded, Adam's royal retinue prepared to ascend the mountain's summit for the crowning in Eden. The procession crossed the narrow promontory, a swell resembling a small mountain dome on the southern slope. Adam and *Chavah* lingered beside the gently flowing Gihon. The cool waters splashed against their skin as they relaxed under the giant canopy of the Tree of the Knowledge of Good and Evil. The tree represented G-d's pure justice; a justice that only G-d could impart to human kings. Adam pondered his royal duties: cultivating and guarding the garden, spreading seed to the four corners of the earth, exercising dominion over the earth, and mediating between G-d and the rest of the human family.

Adam's coronation confirmed his adoption by *Yahweh*, and he was granted the title Son of G-d. The covenant was now firmly established between Father and Son. The garden served as the royal grant of land — legally passed to the son as his inheritance. As Vice-regent, Adam ruled from the garden as a benevolent king responsible for maintaining order. The fertility of the land, as well as the social and political stability, was contingent on Adam's rulings in the legal realm. Unrighteous decisions affected nature; violations brought drought, famine, earthquakes, pestilence, and cosmic upheaval. Under the terms of the covenant, Adam was forbidden to eat fruit from the Tree of Knowledge. The fruit contained seed, which, when ingested, poisoned humans and caused their death.

Adam relished his angelic-like status. Clothed in white light, his garments reflected the worship of G-d to all of the creation. He girded his loins with a belt of finely twisted linen embroidered with sky blue and crimson thread. He also wore a *choshen*, a linen breastplate for righteous judgment, woven with threads of gold, blue, and crimson, and filled with a covering of precious stones: ruby, topaz, diamond, beryl, onyx, jasper, sapphire, turquoise, and emerald. Adam would soon be crowned with a *netzer* of pure gold engraved with the words "Holy to the Lord." Worn from ear to ear, across his forehead, it resembled the bow in the sky. Adam, the image-bearer, stood in awe of the royal mantle he wore, a mantle conferred by a merciful king. As Vice-regent and one who exemplified the authority of G-d, Adam was called to subdue the earth while exercising justice. Adam basked in G-d's glory and the blessings of a special covenantal relationship that mirrored the unity of Heaven and Earth; he was the human image of creation's temple.

Without warning, a mysterious figure appeared from behind the tree — hissing in Adam and *Chavah's* direction,

"Did the One True G-d really tell you not to eat from any of the trees in this most luxuriant garden of your king?" Adam knew the voice: Inanna, Uruk's snake goddess! Adam had served this queen of heaven and mother goddess of the grapevine as the chief gardener in Mesopotamia. Burning with jealousy, Inanna traversed the world over — intent on restoring Adam to his rightful position as heir and king of Uruk. Adam had failed to subdue Inanna, and now the shiny snake goddess would subdue Adam in the garden. He had allowed this enemy from the field to enter the sacred space and dishonor his G-d. Instead of guarding and protecting the garden from chaos and disorder, he welcomed it.

Inanna's razor-sharp tongue went to work. *Chavah*, mesmerized by the glittering gold goddess bedecked in fine jewels, succumbed to her deceptions. Inanna whispered, "G-d knows that when you eat of the tree, your eyes will be opened and you will be like G-d, knowing good and evil! You most assuredly won't die." *Chavah* fell prey to her flattery; she trusted in Inanna's empty promises of secret wisdom and power to turn humans into gods. Enticed by the rich, velvety-coated figs suspended from the tree's branches, *Chavah* grabbed hold of the fruit. She "took" and "ate" and presented it to Adam who followed suit. He ate the sweet, succulent fruit — and with it the myriad of seeds. The goddess seemed appeased. She congratulated herself on winning the victory over the One True G-d; she had persuaded Adam to break the covenant. She now expected Adam to take his "rightful" position as King over Uruk and once again worship her. Creation began to reel and groan in agony, despairing from the effects of Adam's disobedience. Celestial bodies listed in the heavens; cataclysmic activity showered the earth. A violent earthquake split the earth to its core; fire rained down from the heavens, and choking smoke rose up from the abyss.

Lightning flashed through thick clouds; G-d appeared as a fiery column walking in the garden. Powerful thunderclaps shook the mountain; the echo pierced through the cavernous rows of trees. Adam and *Chavah* trembled uncontrollably at the sound of His footsteps. The guardians became trespassers — enemies inside the camp. Together they searched for protection from the wrath that would surely follow. Crouching behind the giant leaves of the Tree of Knowledge, barely breathing, they clung tightly to its muscular trunk. The serpent goddess continued her taunts. She mocked Adam for his nakedness and gloated over the success of her mission. By breaking the covenant, Adam declared himself a god, sitting in the seat of the gods, reigning over the earth as a god. By eating the fruit, the image-bearing king proclaimed himself equal with G-d — turning himself into a man-made idol to be worshipped.

Chavah tugged loose a giant fig leaf and wove a *chagar* (apron) for hanging weapons. Tucking the hem of their robes into the apron, they girded their loins in preparation for divine retribution. Adam and *Chavah* brought shame and dishonor to their Creator and allowed the sacred space to become contaminated through the wiles of the serpent. Exile would be necessary for the garden to heal and take its rest. The voice of G-d thundered; it spewed out flames of fire. "You are human, mortal — even if you think you are god."

Inanna, the serpent goddess, was forcibly removed from the garden sanctuary — condemned to "walk" on her belly — compelled to take a docile position. She remained pregnant with all the pleasures and desires of the flesh — desires that when conceived give birth to sin. From her womb, seeds of chaos, confusion, and death were sown that reproduced the nature of a beast in men. Adam, once the priestly image of his Creator, allowed himself to be ruled by unrelenting appetites. He exchanged the glory of G-d for an idol of himself. Adam lamented that the kings of the earth, who plotted evil, would now conspire against him.

In a fit of rage, Adam threw down the keys to the garden as

he departed through the gate into the field. He blamed *Chavah* who in turn blamed the serpent. They argued, they cursed, they tore each other apart with words of insult and condemnation. Adam refused to admit responsibility. *Chavah* threatened to return to the alluvial plains of the east and renounce her kingdom citizenship. Adam begged her to stay.

With nostrils flaring and refusing defeat, Inanna determined she would destroy any vestige of G-d's image in the field. She marshaled her troops for battle against the throne of the One True G-d. She whistled. Her massive array of soldiers marched from the east towards Eden's mountain like a locust swarm. Swords were drawn; bronze shields were raised and readied for battle. The captain of the guard awaited Inanna's orders.

Adam admitted he had allowed the serpent to gain entry. Despondent, he clenched the handful of herbs and spices for the incense and the heirloom seeds he carried out of the garden. He hung his head in shame; emotions churning, Adam wept. Cast out from the garden, Adam and *Chavah* became slaves to the ground — forced to labor as if they were providing food for the gods.

Terror rose in his heart. Adam begged *Yahweh*, "Correct me, but with your justice, not in your anger, lest you bring me to nothing." The weight of his actions pressed in hard. The unrelenting guilt was unbearable. Held captive, tormented by his thoughts and feelings, Adam cried out in pain for deliverance and release: "Turn your ear to me. Bring my soul up from *she'ol*. Keep me alive, so I don't descend into the pit. Rescue me quickly, for I have suffered the disgrace of my disobedience. Be a rock for me, and free me from the net of the nations that will cause me to disappear. See my affliction and the deep troubles of my soul. Don't hand me over to the serpent's kingdom. My eyes are wasting away with grief along with my body and my soul. My life is consumed with sorrow and death. My bones are decaying. I am a broken vessel. May I be released from the devastation I have caused, O Lord, please hear my pleas."

Yahweh his G-d, who loved him with an everlasting love, spoke words of comfort and healing. "The life your parents gave you is precious. A promised seed will come and bring you comfort in your misery, and relief in your toil, even though the ground is still cursed. His name will be *Noach*; he will provide repentance and rest to you and your seed. He will console those who mourn in *Tziyon* and will soothe all the earth's waste places and make the wilderness like Eden once again. Earth, now in a state of chaos, will be like the garden of G-d again. Joy and gladness will be found on the holy hill. Thanksgiving and gratitude will become a soul's sweet melody."

Inanna promoted all manner of aberrant behavior in humankind — encouraging her king-seed to stir up chaos. Her goal: fill the earth with detestable idolatry, corrupt the image of G-d, and torment His servants. She squealed with delight whenever His image-bearers indulged in the works of the flesh: sexual immorality, impurity, indecency, idolatry, witchcraft, hostility, strife, jealousy, rage, selfish ambition, dissension, factions, envy, drunkenness, carousing... Her wild beasts replaced the *shalom* of the Kingdom, and turmoil — the fruit that was consummated in idolatry — filled the earth. She transformed herself into a shiny, golden idol that the nations and their rulers happily worshipped.

Two cherubim stood at the threshold of the garden gate waving flaming swords in six directions. There Adam would build a stone altar using the blueprint provided by *Elohim* so that he and his progeny could draw near. The man-made, stone altar resembled the tripartite model of the cosmos — patterned after the heavens, the earth, and the sea. The bottom, the *azarah ketanah*, was like a small courtyard. In the middle, the *soviv* (meaning surround) was called the *azarah gedolah* or large courtyard. The *Har El*, Mount of G-d, was the roof that accommodated a perpetually burning fire. And so, G-d confirmed a blood covenant with Adam at the entrance to the garden before sending him into the field to work the *adamah* (ground).

✡   ✡   ✡

Adam and *Chavah* settled outside *Urushalim* close to the entrance of the garden. It was chosen for a divine purpose; it served as a civilizing influence on the social, economic, and political world of the ancients. Adam's family dwelled in the pastoral area surrounding the city where livestock could be raised for the service of the altar. The family kept their flocks as close as possible to the Gihon because of its continuous water supply and good grazing land. Adam remembered how the Mesopotamians worshipped their burgeoning cities; to them, civilized life was a gift given to men from the gods. G-d continued to bless Adam and his family in their agricultural pursuits — the true foundation for the success of the city.

Adam dug a cistern for water storage adjacent to a small cedar grove, and he plastered the cistern walls with clay. He and his sons erected a simple two-story limestone structure for his growing family — complete with a central stone fireplace for chilly *Urushalim* nights. Giant cedar beams stretched across the roof with long willow branches placed in between. Stone steps towards the back of the house led to an upper room set aside for prayer. Olive groves and vineyards were planted from the seed Adam acquired in the garden; the fruit provided food in abundance for the entire family. Adam passed on his gardening vocation to Cain, his firstborn, to cultivate the ground and present the first fruit at the altar. Adam and *Chavah* handed the responsibility for raising livestock to their second born son, Abel, who became the family's chief shepherd.

In addition to his agricultural responsibilities, Adam labored tirelessly as a skilled artisan. He chiseled out small stones from a large rock for an altar at the high place on the mountain. Once the hewn stones fit tightly together, the sons attached the stone ramp. Twice daily, in the morning and in the evening, Abel slaughtered a ram from the flock, cut it into nine pieces, and threw the parts on the altar atop the perpetual flame. He collected the blood in a special vessel, sprinkled it on the horns at the altar's four corners, and splashed the remaining blood against the lower section. Every seventh day, Cain, the firstborn, removed the bloodstains and restored the altar to its original color — a job he came to abhor.

Elohim delighted in the sweet-smelling aroma from the *Tamid Korban Olah* (daily elevation offering) as the fire consumed the burnt offering. It reminded Abel of his wickedness; he was grateful for the atonement — the divine solution G-d provided for his sinful state. The first sacrifice was offered each morning which allowed the entire family to draw close to G-d. Thick smoke rose up in a column; it connected Earth to Heaven. Only the skins remained of the animal. The hides were tanned outside the camp and used for writing materials, garments, sandals and shoes, and even *nods* — skin bottles for storing and transporting liquids.

Cain brought his *minchah* (grain or first fruit offering) early one morning before Abel offered up the *Tamid Korban Olah*. As a result, G-d did not look favorably upon Cain's offering; it was not presented at the designated time. Cain became enraged at this perceived injustice. *Why must Abel always approach first?* Cain was, after all, the firstborn son, the future chief gardener, and next in line to rule. Jealousy turned to hate which festered. While standing in the field before the altar, Cain rose up and killed Abel. When G-d asked Cain of the whereabouts of his brother, he responded heatedly, "I do not know! Am I the guardian of my brother?" Cain had cut off Abel's potential seed from the dynasty. As the blood seeped slowly into the nearly impenetrable ground, the crimson-stained earth opened its mouth; the blood drained into a narrow channel and pooled underneath the altar. Cain searched for somewhere to hide the body. Chiseling out a section of the hard limestone rock on the steep slopes just outside *Urushalim*, in a place called the "field of blood," he buried his brother in a cave. Abel's righteous blood would eventually be avenged.

G-d placed a sign on Cain to protect him from being killed. Instead of death, he bore the label of an uncivilized nomad and was seen as a threat to sophisticated society. A wild man, a beast in the field, he became the rallying cry for the despised and the feared. Cain would never work again as a farmer or enjoy the freedom that comes from cultivating seed. He would be permanently enslaved in the nations where he would ultimately disappear. Cain lost his sense of purpose, and so he wasted away like his brother, Abel.

Adam and *Chavah* both grieved the loss of their sons. Adam knew his wife again, and she bore a son and named him Seth, "For G-d has appointed another seed for me instead of Abel, whom Cain killed." The line of the kings would continue through Seth until *the* Messiah came and restored the broken covenant, cleansed from sin, and defeated the serpent's mighty army.

When Adam broke the covenant with G-d, he caused a permanent rupture in the relationship between father and son in the natural realm. The murder of Abel continued the downward spiral. Adam's progeny found that life in the field impeded the bond between fathers and sons which resulted in ongoing family dysfunction. It would affect every family for millennia to come. Fathers and sons would struggle to build and maintain trust and intimacy. Sons would be driven by anger and rebellion against their fathers because of neglect. Fathers would respond against sons for failing to live up to their expectations. An inability to connect would lead to devastating consequences for families and nations and for society at large. The image of G-d in men had been drastically diminished.

The serpent figure drove the rulers of the earth in their quest for control of the world. They sought to crush, intimidate, and persecute the weak and vulnerable. Corrupt despots continually rose up to ravage the earth for personal gain — exerting power, influence, and control not only over the masses of humanity but against the One True G-d and His anointed ones. The two kingdoms were constantly in conflict. The adversary became obsessed with usurping the throne of G-d and installing a representative — a reality that was repeated through the empires of Egypt, Assyria, Babylon, Persia, Greece, and Rome. Only G-d's image-bearers could stand against these forces of tyranny but at the cost of becoming martyrs themselves. At one moment in history, in first-century Israel, evil converged on a tree — the barbarity of the Roman empire, the corruption and exploitation of the ruling class of the land of Israel, and the violent political factions all created unrest and chaos for the earth. The Second Adam suffered and was crucified at the place where Heaven and Earth meet. "[T]he Messiah is Israel's guarantor; he has undertaken suffering to atone for Israel's sins in order to shorten the exile" (*Yalkut Shimoni* 499). Along with Messiah's burial and resurrection from the dead, he overthrew the mighty kings of the earth.

Exile

> My tent is destroyed and all my ropes are snapped.
> My Children are gone from me and are no more.
> No one is left to stretch out my tent
> Or set up my tent curtains.
>
> (JEREMIAH 10.20)

The story of Adam's exile from the garden became the story of Israel's exile from the Promised Land. Adam's disobedience caused creation to unravel; the earth felt the effects first. "The expulsion of Adam and Eve from the garden, and the garden's bringing forth thorns and thistles, is the equivalent in terms of the whole human race of the expulsion of Israel from the land" (ed. J. Scott 2017: 71). Fretheim explained that the people's sin had put an intolerable strain on the land and so it needed time to recover. The sabbatical years, like the weekly Sabbath, provided rest from human interference (2005: 139). He added that failure to observe this practice resulted in negative effects, that is, the removal of the people from the land. The field needed redemption — as did men; both the land and mankind experienced a liberation every "seventh." Exile allowed the sacred space to "rest" from the contamination caused by Israel's idolatry.

Adam enjoyed the protection his covenant relationship with *Yahweh* provided. Violating the commandment not to eat fruit from the Tree of Knowledge resulted in his exile from the garden — a separation akin to the dissolution of marriage. Adam became *garash* (divorced) from the rich soil that sprouted trees to produce fruit in abundance. Stripped bare, Adam and *Chavah* became vulnerable to the field's hostile environment: the consequences of breaking the covenant. Now, they were removed from a place of honor and were exiled to a place of disgrace; they had played the harlot refusing to cover their shame.

During the Babylonian exile, Jeremiah reminded the people how they had sprawled under every green tree like a prostitute. How they had worshipped on every high hill! Israel's harlotry led to the destruction of the central sanctuary and exile to foreign lands. Ezekiel (23) provides a very graphic picture of Samaria and Jerusalem prostituting themselves to Assyria and Babylon respectively. G-d gave them over to their lusts. He exiled them into the very nations with whom they had committed adultery. "If a man divorces his wife and she leaves him to be with another man, will he return to her again? Would not such a land be totally polluted? You are a prostitute with many lovers. Now are you returning to Me?" (Jer. 3.1). Israel continually ran after the gods of foreign lands; at home, they imitated the practices of the nations where they once lived.

Because of the many fornications of the elegant prostitute, the mistress of sorceries, who sells nations by her fornications, and clans through her sorceries — Behold, I am against you — it is a declaration of *Adonai Tzva'ot* — I will lift your skirts over your face, I will show the nations your nakedness and kingdoms your disgrace.

(NAHUM 3.4,5)

Adam soon discovered a dry and thirsty land in desperate need of water for both plants and people — a land where Adam's family would continually struggle to regain their humanity and where death would seek to destroy worthless flesh. They became like beasts in the field who lacked the image-bearing form the man was originally given. Chief among the beasts was the serpent, whose existence depended on corrupting the image of G-d by preying upon G-d's image-bearers and manipulating the world's rulers and princes. The serpent's image mirrored that of the great sea monsters in the deep who ruled over chaos from their thrones. G-d's image-bearers groaned under tyranny — oppressed and enslaved by the world's ruling elites. *Elohim*, in His mercy and compassion, instructed Adam to build an altar of stone in the field at the entrance to the garden. There, he and his descendants could draw near to the place of G-d's Presence until the King of kings and Lord of lords finally conquered the world's tyrants and liberated His children for eternity.

In the beginning, it took seven *yamim* (days) to build G-d's Cosmic House. He rested on the seventh having brought order out of non-order and function out of formlessness. Israel's agricultural cycle is patterned after the seven days of creation: Unleavened Bread is a seven-day festival, followed by the seven weeks of counting the *Omer* until *Shavuot* (meaning sevens). *Rosh HaShanah*, the head of the year and the day of the blowing of the shofar, begins the first day of the seventh month. *Sukkot* is the seven-day festival for the ingathering of the harvest. Every seven years, a *sh'mittah* is celebrated to give the land rest; no sowing, planting, or reaping are allowed (Lev. 25.20). Every fiftieth year, called the *Yovel* or year of release (the year following seven cycles of seven years), the land is returned to its original owner, and all slaves are set free. Seventy years were determined for Israel's exile in Babylon so the land could rest and recover from Israel's idolatry. Ultimately, when the heavens and the earth unite on a *Yovel*, the earth's ownership will be transferred back to *its* rightful owner — the King of the Universe.

Exile is a chaos-type environment corresponding to the primordial condition before creation. It is described in Scripture as a wasteland, a parched place, a dry and thirsty land, a desert or wilderness, an empty pit, and a dry cistern cut off from rivers of living water. The book of Lamentations (an expression of grief for the destruction of the Temple) compares Israel's sin with violating the laws of ritual purity: "Jerusalem has greatly sinned — therefore, she has become *niddah*" [removed from the camp]" (1.8). In practical terms, a woman was *niddah*, or separated from her husband, during her monthly cycle because of the death of her potential offspring. An immersion restored her purity and enabled her to re-enter the camp. This was not a moral issue, for she hadn't sinned. It was due to the need to protect the sacred space from the contamination of death. Returning to a state of ritual purity required cleansing in water, and this was required by one approaching the King.

Genesis *Rabbah* (21.8) compares the expulsion of Adam and Eve from Eden to the destruction of the Temple. Israel's idolatry produced cataclysmic outcomes: famine, plagues, pestilence, earthquakes, and wars which made it difficult for the seed to sprout and take root. "Their root will be like rot, and their blossom will go up like dust. For they have rejected the Torah of *Adonai*" (Is. 5.24). A barren woman was a metaphor for the primordial state of chaos and disorder. Three things never brought nor were filled with satisfaction: the grave, the barren womb, and the dry earth (Prov. 30. 15,16). When the matriarchs, who were barren, finally became pregnant, the birth of their offspring (the kings) was a declaration of new creation corresponding to the birth of the Kingdom.

Why did Jacob and his sons go down to Egypt (the world) to live in exile? Jacob instructed his sons to take some of the best products of the land and bring an offering to the man, Joseph, in Egypt: balsam, a little honey, gum, myrrh, pistachios and almonds (Gen. 43.11). This suggests the trees in Canaan still produced fruit. However, Jacob sent ahead his ten sons to Egypt to buy grain so they would "live" (Gen. 42.1,2). The family was eventually sent to Egypt — the consequence due Jacob's sons for having removed Joseph, their co-heir, from the Promised Land by selling him into slavery (the worst judgment possible in the ancient world). And so, Jacob and his family, numbering seventy, lived as foreigners in Egypt. Once the entire family reunited, they became "fruitful and increased abundantly, multiplied and grew exceedingly numerous — so the land was filled with them" (Ex. 1.7).

Joseph, when raised up from the pit, served as Vice-regent over Egypt to preserve the grain seed — the *Benai Israel*, the sons of G-d. In time, a new pharaoh ascended the throne who did not "know" Joseph, that is, he refused to recognize Joseph's position of authority under the rule of G-d. Israel — forced to abandon their agricultural and shepherding lifestyle — built monuments from brick to the new pharaoh. "Abandoning the commands of the Lord they [united] themselves with *Beliar*. Giving up agriculture, they [followed] their evil schemes" (*Testament of Issachar* 6.1–2). Fearful of losing power, Pharaoh set task masters to enslave the children of Israel, to kill their seed, and to hinder them from reproducing and spreading seed. "They [Egyptians] worked them [children of Israel] harshly with mortar and brick, doing all sorts of work in the fields" (Ex. 1.14).

G-d delivered Israel from Pharaoh's army then birthed the nation through the waters of *Yam Suph* (Sea of Reeds). What followed was the climax of the Exodus — the restoration of Creation in the raising up of the Tabernacle and the creation week being repeated. In the wilderness, G-d provided the raw materials necessary to assemble the Tabernacle: "I will plant in the wilderness the cedar and the acacia tree, the myrtle and the oil tree; I will set in the desert the cypress tree and the pine and the box tree together" (Is. 41.19). The architectural language that described creation is tied to the Tabernacle's construction: All the work of the Tabernacle, the Tent of Meeting, was *kallah* (completed) like the heavens and earth. The new nation burst forth as a sprout from the ground; once the sea split, the waters gathered, and the dry land appeared (Gen. 1.9,10).

In Ezekiel's temple, "Water was flowing out from under the threshold of the House eastward... down from under the right side of the House" (Ezek. 47.1). In the Tabernacle, water gushed from a rock — mirroring streams flowing in the wilderness and rivers coursing through wastelands. When the captives returned to Zion, the formerly dry places became a well-watered garden where roses blossomed.

> Here I am, doing a new thing; Now it is springing up — do you not know about it? I will surely make a way in the desert, rivers in the wasteland...I give waters in the desert, rivers in the wilderness, to give drink to My chosen people, so they might declare My praise
>
> (ISAIAH 43.19)

Israel was also a watered plant rooted in the garden's rich soil, bearing seed, and producing offspring; the genealogies in the Bible represent this creation ideal. The Gospel of Matthew begins, "A book of the Genesis of Jesus Christ, Son of David" (Beale and Carson 2007: 2). Based on the pattern of *toldot* (bringing forth children) of the heavens and earth (Gen. 2.4),

Matthew chronicles the generations from Abraham to *Yeshua* the Messiah. The three groups of fourteen generations listed emphasize the exile as a stopping and starting point. Forty-two generations are listed in all — related to the forty-two camps in the wilderness where the Tabernacle stood "in their midst" (Num. 33). According to N.T. Wright, six sevens (the six days of creation) would pass before the exile ended. He further explains that this is what Daniel the Prophet is speaking of (9.24) and that *Yeshua* was the seventh seven who came to rescue Israel from its "long exile" (2012: 71). The genealogy extended from Abraham to David (14), from David to the Babylonian exile (14), and from the Babylonian exile to *Yeshua* (14). Perhaps this is also related to the numerical value for David's name: *dalet, vav, dalet* is 14. According to John Walton, Mesopotamian genealogies were mostly royal; they believed the kings were the image of their god's power and reign (2009: 44).

When sins were forgiven in the Temple — the place of the Presence of G-d, the exile ended. The destruction of the Second Temple came after *Yeshua* rose from the dead. NT Wright explains that the Jews of the first century saw Roman domination as a continuation of the exile.

> Most Jews of this period, it seems, would have answered the question of 'where are we?' in language, which, reduced to its simplest form, meant: we are still in exile. They believed that, in all the senses which mattered, Israel's exile was still in progress. Although she had come back from Babylon, the glorious message of the prophets remained unfulfilled. Israel still remained in thrall to foreigners; worse, Israel's god had not returned to Zion.
>
> (WRIGHT 1992: 268–269)

Yeshua's encounter with the Samaritan woman at the well (John 4) draws out this theme. He agreed with her, "For you've had five husbands, and the man you have now isn't your husband" (Jn. 4.18). *Yeshua* compared Samaria's (the ten northern tribes) bond with the five foreign powers and called them husbands: Egypt, Assyria, Babylon, Persia, and Greece. Rome was the sixth "man" who wasn't a legitimate husband. The Samaritans claimed to be the true children of Israel, descendants of the tribe of Joseph (Ephraim and Manasseh), who remained faithful to the Torah of Moses. (There is a tradition that 300 priests and 300 rabbis once gathered in the temple court in Jerusalem to curse the Samaritans with all the curses in the Law of Moses.)

Like Israel, the shoot, the Messiah, sprouted forth from the earth to become a great tree who would build G-d's House. Messiah *Yeshua* was the *Tzemach* (sprout), the new creation, the new temple where G-d's Presence dwelled. "To whom is the arm of *Adonai* revealed? For before him he grew up like a young plant, like a root out of dry ground" (Is. 53.2).

> At least there is hope for a tree — if it is cut down it will sprout again, and its shoots will not cease. Though its roots grow old in the earth and its stump dies in the dry ground, at the scent of water it will bud and sprout sprigs like a new plant.
>
> (JOB 14.7)

The parable of the mustard seed tells of the Kingdom of G-d. "Though the smallest of all seeds in the earth, yet when planted it grows up and becomes the largest of all the herbs. It puts forth big branches, so the birds of the air can nest in its shade" (Mark 4.31,32). A comparison is being made to the family of Jacob, which the Prophet Amos calls small (7.2), and to Bethlehem, *Ephrathah*, who is small among the clans of Judah. From them will come the ruler of Israel (Micah 5.2).

Freedom from exile required the removal of detestable idols and payment for the forgiveness of sin (made in the place G-d placed His Presence) so that the land could heal.

Now I will restore Jacob from exile, when I have compassion on the whole House of Israel. I will be zealous for My Holy Name. They will bear the shame and all their disloyalty by which they broke faith [covenant] with Me, when they were living securely in their land, with no one making them afraid. When I have brought them back from the peoples and have gathered them out of the enemies' lands, I will be sanctified in them in the eyes of many nations. Then they will know that I am *Adonai* their G-d, since it was I who caused them to go into exile among the nations and I who will gather them back to their own land. I will never again leave them there. I will never again hide My face from them. For I have poured out My *Ruach* upon the house of Israel.

(EZEKIEL 39.25–29)

When *Yeshua* the Messiah, who is the representative of Israel, fulfills his redemptive work, then the exile of all humanity will be over.

The Field

This land that was desolate has become like the garden of Eden; the wasted, desolate, and ruined cities are fortified and inhabited.

(EZEKIEL 36.35)

Adam and *Chavah* enjoyed a special kinship with the *adamah* (ground) until they broke the covenant and were estranged. "After the expulsion from the Garden the ground [sprouted] thorns and thistles and Adam [was] relegated to eating plants of the field, because *Yahweh* [had] cursed the ground. This connotes hardship and pain in the ordinary world...the perfect creation has been rolled back into chaos" (George and George 2014: 119). Affliction and distress accompanied them as they cultivated the unrelenting ground. According to the sages, to tend a field really meant to enslave it. To grow crops, men came along and enslaved the earth, and forced pieces of land to produce.

The field lay to the east of the garden — in the opposite direction of Eden — a world of chaos where beasts and wild animals lived and where the serpent ruled over men. Jackals and wild beasts became metaphors for Israel's enemies — foreigners who attacked Israel and turned the "land" into a stronghold for thorns and thistles. "Remind the nations, proclaim over Jerusalem! Besiegers are soon coming from a far country, raising their voice against the cities of Judah. Like keepers of a field they surround her, because she has been rebellious against Me" (Jer. 4.17). When the Assyrian army came against Ahaz, King of Judah (father of Hezekiah), Isaiah warned that every place where there were a thousand vines worth a thousand silver shekels would become briars and thorns (Is. 7.23). "But [the earth] which produces thorns and thistles, it is worthless and near to being cursed — its end is to be burned over" (Heb. 6.8).

The serpent's home was the field. Cain murdered his brother in the field (Gen 4:8). Esau, Jacob's twin brother who sold his birthright for stew, was a man of the field (Gen. 25.27). *Akeldama*, Aramaic for "field of blood," was named for the *adamah*: the ground's reddish color from the spilling of human blood. Located just outside Jerusalem on the steep slope of Mount Zion, burial caves were chiseled into the limestone rock. The caves housed the remains of affluent Jewish families and those belonging to the aristocracy of Jerusalem in the First and Second Temple period.

According to the book of Acts (1.19), Judas purchased the field and then fell headfirst (prone in Greek) in such a way that his intestines "splattered out." His swollen belly violently ruptured — which led to his death. The woman "suspected of adultery" (called the *Sotah*) drank the bitter waters that caused her belly to swell. If found guilty of unfaithfulness, she experienced a miscarriage or the death of her seed (Num. 5.27). A battle continues to play out between the seed of the woman and the seed of the serpent. By the first century, the serpent in the field morphed into the image of the devil; both came to represent the kings and rulers of the earth which included the ruling elites of Israel — just like thorn bushes and briers who snag the innocent and the ram caught in the thicket as the substitute for Isaac (Gen. 22.13).

Beasts of the field represented foreign rulers who subjugated Israel, oppressed the poor, and tyrannized their citizens as well as those they conquered. Within the nation of Israel, a curse came upon the land for those leaders who violated the commandments of G-d. Wicked kings from both Israel and Judah ruled with an iron fist, and without justice, compassion, or mercy. They were as weeds sprouting up in the field! The weeds were described as the sons of the evil one (Matt. 13.38). Judgment came upon the people because their leaders violated the covenant. "I looked at the earth and behold it was deserted and desolate…I looked and behold the fruitful field was a wilderness and all of its cities were in ruins" (Jer. 4.23–28).

Even David recognized his beast nature. In speaking of his contemporaries, the kings and ruling elites of his day, he recognized how he envied them in his heart when he saw their prosperity and how they never experienced humanity's trouble. David observed they seemed at ease while amassing great wealth. He was greatly troubled by this and so cried out, "I entered the Sanctuary of G-d and perceived their end. When my heart was embittered and I was pierced in my heart, I was brutish and ignorant. I was like a beast before you" (Ps. 73.17,21,22).

In the field (which is the world), *Yeshua*, son of David, explained there *would be* tribulation, but that He had overcome the world. The servant promised to restore the Covenant of

Shalom (peace) and deliver his children from the wild beasts. That required removing the evil beasts from the land so the people could dwell safely in the wilderness where the trees of the field would yield produce and where Israel's agricultural prowess would become renown (Ezek. 34.25,27–29). "Instead of the thorn bush, a cypress will come up, and instead of briar, a myrtle will come up, and it will be a memorial to *Adonai*, as an everlasting sign that will never be cut off" (Is. 55.13).

"In mythology, including in the ancient Near East and throughout the Bible, such a wild, uncultivated, desert wasteland commonly signifies chaos, the void and nonexistence — the formless modality of pre-creation — and thus parallels in meaning the primordial waters" (George and George 2014: 95). The field was analogous to the primordial, formless void and was related to the desert and the wastelands. Natural laws govern the field. Seed germinates, grows into a plant or tree that creates flowers, and when fertilized produces fruit containing seed for the next generation. Like a man's flesh, plants decay and decompose in the earth, seed dies and lays dormant waiting for the right conditions to germinate — a combination of sunshine, rich soil, and abundant water. "If you walk in My statutes, keep My *Mitzvot* and carry them out, then I will give you rains in their season, the land will yield its crops and the trees of the field will yield their fruit" (Lev. 26.3). "For the earth — having soaked up the rain frequently falling on it — brings forth vegetation useful to those for whom it is farmed; and it shares in G-d's blessing" (Heb. 6.7).

Israel built the Tabernacle, a miniature cosmos, in the pattern of creation. Like Adam, who was also a miniature cosmos, it was formed from the dust of the earth — raised up from dry, desolate ground. For nearly forty years, Israel journeyed through the barren wasteland. However, G-d dwelled in their midst and provided His Life-giving Spirit. His living water gushed from a rock that turned chaos into a well-watered garden of fruit-bearing trees! *Yahweh's* Presence enveloped the camp, preserved them, and caused them to multiply and increase, that is, until their idolatry resulted in the death of an entire generation.

The sages connected the field to the concept of *"si'ach,"* which means prayer or meditation. "Before any plant in the field (*si'ach sadeh*) was in the earth [*eretz*]...the Lord had not caused it to rain and there was no man to till the ground" (Gen. 2:5). Praying in the field was tied to the work of a priest cultivating the earth. According to Rabbi Hirsch, the "one who prays drinks from the source of spiritual life, and then waters and refreshes his inner self to produce a garden of blossoms and flowers." The field remained in a state of chaos and disorder until G-d sent rain — and then a new creation sprouted from the earth. *Yeshua* understood the field was a place of sorrow and sadness, heartbreak and loss — a place where Evil lurks ready to kill, steal, and destroy to prevent the image of G-d from being spread through His image-bearers.

> The one sowing the good seed is the Son of Man, and the field is the world. And the good seed, these are the sons of the kingdom; and the weeds are the sons of the evil one. The enemy who sowed them is the devil, the harvest is the end of the age and the reapers are angels...The Son of Man will send forth his angels and they will gather out of his kingdom all stumbling blocks and those who practice lawlessness.
>
> (MATTHEW 13.38)

Now Ephron's field that is in Machpelah next to Mamre (Hebron) — the field and the cave that is in it, and all the trees that are in the field in all its surrounding territory — was handed over to Abraham as a purchased possession...Afterwards, Abraham buried Sarah his wife in the cave in the field...in the land of Canaan.

(GENESIS 23.17,19)

According to the sages, the cave in Ephron's field led to the Garden in Eden. Sarah was gathered to her forefathers, Adam and *Chavah*, and was buried there to await the resurrection. Machpelah means double; Hebron means companions. Caves in the ancient world represented the inner sanctum of a temple — where Heaven and Earth meet and where two become one. "A cave or tomb inside a mountain was a symbol for the temple's sacred center. Entering the mountain's cave signified entering the earth" (George 2014: 102). The body of *Yeshua*, wrapped in linen and sealed with a mixture of myrrh of aloes, was buried in a new tomb in a garden (Jn. 19.40–42) waiting to be raised up on the third day. Our mothers and fathers will ultimately spring up from the earth to re-create the Creation Temple. Trees that sprouted near the cave replaced the thorn bushes; they were an everlasting sign of the restoration of the House of G-d.

When the new heavens and new earth become one, *kallah* (completed), as in marriage (Rev. 21.1; Is. 66.22), the field/land will be transformed. And so, Isaac waited patiently in the field for his bride to return from exile. "Isaac went out to meditate, strolling in the field at dusk. Then he lifted up his eyes and saw, behold camels were coming. Isaac brought [Rebekah] into the tent of Sarah, his mother, took Rebekah and she became his wife — and he loved her" (Gen. 24.63,67). Isaac called the temple a field. The sages declared that the king (Isaac) would be in the field during the sixth month, Elul — a time for divine mercy conducive to prayer and repentance. Elul forms the anagram, "I am my beloved's, and my beloved is mine" (*Ani l'dodi v'dodi li*). The intense love between Isaac and Rebekah perfectly reflected the relationship between G-d and His people.

CHAPTER FOUR

KINGS

When you come to the land that Adonai your G-d is giving you, possess it and dwell in it, and you say, 'I will set a king over me, like all the nations around me,' You will indeed set over yourselves a king, whom Adonai your G-d chooses. One from among your brothers will be appointed as king over you.
(Deuteronomy 17.14–15a)

The following fictional vignette fills in the gaps of the *Akeidah*: the binding of *Yitzchak* (Gen. 22). According to tradition, the event took place on Mount Moriah: the site of the Temple. However, the Mount of Olives, the mountain to the east of Moriah, was chosen for this particular vignette. The *Rosh* (head) of the Mount of Olives was the location for the offering of the red heifer during the Second Temple period. It was there *Avraham* once pitched his tent, erected an altar, and called on the Name of the Lord (Gen. 12.8). The Mount of Olives was also called the Mount of Anointment for its many olive groves that produced the oil for anointing the kings of Israel.

In the *Akeidah*, *Yitzchak* (Isaac) was offered up as an *olah* (elevation offering) which was usually a burnt offering. However, since *olah* is a feminine noun, it could also refer to the red heifer. Both offerings were completely consumed. During the first century, the heifer was bound with reed grass and laid upon the altar before being slaughtered. After being consumed by fire, its ashes were mixed with water from the Gihon Spring (where Solomon was anointed king). On the third and seventh day, those defiled by corpse uncleanness were sprinkled with the mixture to remove the contamination.

✡   ✡   ✡

As night descended onto the desert camp, *Avraham* peered through the tent opening to check the fire. Evenings were still chilly even as summer approached. He grabbed a few cedar logs, arranged them atop the dying embers, and waited for the dry wood to burst into flames. While warming his hands, *Avraham* reflected on the pivotal moments of his life. He recalled the day he "crossed over" the Jordan River and entered the land of Canaan; he remembered how *Adonai* his G-d had appeared to him on Mount Moriah with the promise that his seed would inherit the land. *Avram* (his name before G-d made a covenant with him) had responded to G-d's promise by building an altar in the place where Adam once served the Lord — outside the boundary of the garden sanctuary. *Avram* had then moved eastward from *Beit El* (House of G-d) to a mountain known for its olive oil. It has been said that from that mountain a dove once plucked an olive leaf from an *etz shemen* (oil tree) to present it to Noah. *Avram* had pitched his tent there and, again, built an altar to *YHWH*.

As he sat, warmed by the fire, *Avraham's* mind drifted back over his life. He remembered "the day" nearly *forty* years earlier, on the *fourteenth* of the first month, when he saw the Divine

Presence passing through the halved animals in the form of a burning torch and a smoking furnace. *Adonai* his G-d had cut a covenant with *Avram* as a father would with his son. *Avram* knew with certainty that the land G-d promised to his descendants was an eternal inheritance — a royal grant based on his loyalty and faithfulness to the One True G-d.

Avraham, now well-advanced in years, thought back to when *Adonai* confirmed he would become the "father" of a multitude of nations through his offspring. *Avram* had experienced some doubt, having no heir at the time, but he had also marveled at G-d's promise that kings would come forth from his loins and Sarah's womb in their old age. A *Brit Milah* (Covenant of Circumcision) sealed the eternal destiny of his seed, and the gift of a new name secured *Avraham's* legal status as king.

Avraham then remembered the dread he felt when G-d made clear his seed would experience bitter exile and enslavement under foreign oppressors in both Canaan and Egypt. This would last *four hundred* years. But *Avraham* took comfort knowing that, in the *fourth* generation, his royal offspring would return to take possession of the land. He considered the significance of the number *four*, which would come to symbolize the natural world — like the *forty* days it takes an embryo to form or the *forty* weeks for the birth of a child. *Avraham* knew *four* meant times of great suffering, hardship, and tribulation followed by new creation: the birth of the Kingdom of Heaven on earth from *his* offspring.

Avraham pondered his move south to the Negev and the town of *Beersheva* (well of seven, oath). Built on the banks of a wadi, the town was strategically located on the main trade route for the caravansaries at the southern edge of prime agricultural land. Well-known for its easy access to abundant underground springs, it was a respite for those traveling through the arid landscape. It was in *Beersheva* that *Avraham* and the King of Gerar, *Avimelech* (my father is King), cut a covenant which gave *Avraham* ownership of the well he had dug as well as the surrounding land. *Avimelech*, for his part, accepted *Avraham's* offer of seven lambs and became a witness to the royal grant. *Avraham*, in response, planted an orchard in *Beersheva* declaring *YHWH* the Everlasting G-d. The orchard was reminiscent of the Eternal's pristine garden, His royal land, in Eden — the center of creation. It was only a short time later, when *Avraham* was 100 years old, that his son *Yitzchak* was born.

Shattering *Avraham's* dream state, *Yitzchak* joined his dad by the fire. The two exchanged smiles as they stood facing the mountains of Jerusalem. Together they prayed, "*Shema Israel Adonai Eloheinu Adonai Echad*" (Hear O Israel the Lord our G-d, the Lord is One), and they added, "*Baruch Shem Kevod Malchuto L'olam V'aed*" (Blessed be the Name of His Glorious Kingdom forever).

A booming voice broke the solitude; it divided into flames of fire and shook the camp. Father and son stood awe-struck. The voice called to *Avraham* who responded, "*Hineini*" (Here I am)! G-d said, "Take your only begotten son, *Yitzchak*, whom you love; go to the land of Moriah, and cause him to ascend as an *olah* (a raised up offering) on one of the mountains." *Yitzchak* only saw the voice; he knew the Divine Presence was in their midst.

Avraham tossed and turned all night. Rising early, still weary from only a few hours of sleep, he hastily made preparations for the three-day journey. He chose two young men from his retinue — trusted servants well acquainted with the peculiarities of the family. *Avraham* chopped the cedar logs into smaller pieces then loaded the donkey with the split wood. *Yitzchak*, who had been sleeping soundly, was awakened by the intermittent brays of the animal. The two young men continued packing up the needed supplies: food, water, oil for light, and weapons for protection.

Avraham, Yitzchak, and the two young men set out

on foot heading north. Initially, they made good time due to the flat terrain. However, once they reached the region bordering the mountains leading up to *Hevron*, the climb proved difficult. The journey became arduous and at times even dangerous. In places the roads were nearly impassable — damaged by the winter rains. They felt threatened by the constant howling of wild animals. The four pressed on — exposed to the elements and in peril from roving bands of marauders. They were visibly relieved when they arrived at the outskirts of *Hevron* without incident. Familiar faces greeted them offering fresh provisions, a place to spend the night, and clean water from the local cistern for washing and drinking.

As the sun's first rays appeared above the horizon, *Avraham* set his face towards Jerusalem. He instructed his two young men to remain by the Cave of Machpelah — the burial site for Adam and *Chavah* (Eve) and long considered the entrance to the Garden paradise. *Yitzchak* offered to carry what was needed for the remainder of the journey. *Avraham* loaded the split wood onto *Yitzchak's* back but carried the fire and the knife himself. The son wondered aloud where they would find a lamb for the *olah*; *Avraham* re-assured him that G-d would provide an animal.

Confident in their mission, father and son ascended as *one* to the place where the Lord "would be seen." The incline was steep and the terrain uneven. *Avraham* found himself out of breath at times, but he lifted his eyes to the mountains and knew help would come from the Lord. He knew *Adonai Tzva'ot* (Lord of Hosts) would protect them from evil and watch over them. *Avraham* sensed they were entering another dimension of time and space, where the Divine Presence enveloped them in the shelter of His wings. Transcending the natural world, they entered a holy sphere, a unique place, situated between heaven and earth.

Avraham rebuilt the altar he had erected years earlier.

It was in ruins — its dust-covered stones strewn over the ground. He carefully slid the un-hewn stones back into place to create four walls with a flat surface on top. Then he constructed a ramp. *Yitzchak* watched silently as his father completed the task and rededicated the altar. *Avraham* found some cedarwood to fuel the offering. Then, like priests before him, he stood atop the altar and arranged the wood in the shape of a small tower — wider at the bottom and narrower at the top. He left a few small holes to allow the air to circulate.

Avraham then bound his son with cords of reed grass. *Yitzchak*, tearing up, asked why his father had forsaken him. *Avraham* tied his son's hands to his feet behind him and carefully positioned him atop the wood. The son's head was aimed toward the south with his face to the west; the father stood facing west towards Mount Moriah.

Avraham, overcome with emotion and barely breathing, fought back tears. He stared intently towards the western mountain — to the place where the Divine Presence rested. Grabbing the sharp knife in his right hand, he lifted it to his shoulder then steadied his left hand to catch the blood. The son gazed up at the sky, saw the heavens split open, and heard an angel chorus singing praises: "Worthy is the ram who was slain to receive power and wealth, wisdom and might, honor and glory and blessing forever!" Just as *Avraham* was ready to perform the *shechita* (ritual slaughter) and slit the son's throat, the Angel of the Lord called out, "*Avraham, Avraham,* do not send forth your hand against the young man nor do anything to him. I know that you are a G-d Fearer, from *YHWH's* royal line, since you have not withheld your son, your only son, from me." Relief flooded *Avraham's* soul, and he took comfort in the angel's words.

A light breeze rose. Olive leaves rustled behind *Avraham*. He spun around and beheld a dark brown, muscular ram — its horns, *the* symbol of royal power, were intertwined in the thorns of an olive tree. *Avraham* envisioned holy oil filling up the ram's horns then being poured over his son's head. Overcome with joy, he named the place, *Adonai Yireh*, "the Lord will be seen." The Angel of the Lord spoke again: "Because you did not withhold your son, your only son, I will richly bless you and multiply your seed as the stars of heaven and the sand on the seashore. In your seed, all the nations of the earth will be blessed." *Avraham* understood he was releasing his son, *Yitzchak*, to *Adonai* to become the anointed king, the *mashiach* (messiah)!

Avraham bound the ram on the altar. He slit its throat in one swift motion with his right hand and received the blood in his left. With his index finger, he sprinkled blood seven times as he faced west towards the *Beit El* (House of G-d). He descended the ramp, lit the cedarwood, and watched as the animal was consumed. The pungent smell of the *olah* lingered as the smoke subsided. All that remained were the ashes. *Avraham* understood that in suffering G-d would provide the perfect substitute. He swept up the ashes and left them in a heap at the base of the altar.

Avraham picked up his knife and descended the mountain alone. Physically exhausted and emotionally spent, he was anxious to return to his wife, Sarah, who remained in *BeerSheva*. She had expressed grave doubts about the journey. As he traveled, *Avraham* prayed that, in times of exile and oppression, his descendants would remember the binding of *Yitzchak*. He prayed the binding would restore the broken covenant and renew his family's relationship with the King of the Universe.

He greeted his two young men who were still camped by the Cave of Machpelah. As the three traveled towards *Beersheva*, *Avraham* never discussed what happened on the mountain. The young men, who secretly wondered why *Yitzchak* had not returned with his father, never asked.

Yitzchak stood transfixed in the Presence of the

Almighty — shielded in a world beyond time — secreted in heaven's Holy of Holies. Smoke-filled clouds of aromatic myrrh shrouded the sacred space. Seated at the right hand of the Heavenly King was His Eternal High Priest, the One whose sprinkled blood restored Creation's broken covenant — even before the foundation of the world. *Yitzchak* was transfixed by the sapphire glow radiating from the firmament. He observed the generations of mankind woven into the heavenly curtain. Now he understood! His binding was a precursor for the One who would permanently restore the breach in the covenant. His binding cemented the relationship between king and servant, father and son, and ultimately between Heaven and Earth. His binding in the natural world foreshadowed the eternal. He saw a ram slain, raised up, anointed, and enthroned as King of Kings and Son of G-d!

> **Author's note: The Bible is not clear which offering Isaac represented. It is possible the binding is connected to three different offerings: the Passover lamb, the burnt offering, and/or the red heifer. Exodus *Rabbah* (15.11) links the *Akeidah* (the binding of Isaac) with the offering of the Passover lamb. The book of *Jubilees* (17.15, 18.3,18–19) states the redemption of Isaac took place on Passover. Pesikta *Rabbati* (37) explains how the patriarchs will rise from their graves in Nisan (Passover season) to pay homage to the suffering Messiah. Targum *Neofiti* to Leviticus (22.27) suggests all sacrificial lambs are symbolic of Isaac — including the daily elevation (burnt) offerings. The burnt offering was often a ram on special days such as Shabbat, the New Moon festival, Passover, and New Year's. Most commentaries state the *Akeidah* was an offering tied to *Rosh HaShanah*, the Jewish New Year and the blowing of the ram's horn. The coronation of the king is a central theme for *Rosh Ha*Shanah; blowing the shofar was part of the enthronement ritual. This

entire event seems to foreshadow the suffering servant, *Yeshua*, crucified at Passover, raised up, and crowned king at *Rosh HaShanah*.

Only Begotten Son

The *Akeidah* or binding of *Yitzchak*/Isaac (Genesis 22) is one of the Bible's best-known stories and *the* most important to the Jewish people. It is part of the liturgy that is read daily in the morning and at *Rosh HaShanah* (New Year). An intriguing story, certainly! But it makes little sense to the modern mind. How could a merciful G-d ask a man to kill his own son? For what purpose? Depictions of Abraham offering up his son run the gamut in art, music, literature, and even popular culture. Consider Bob Dylan's song "Highway 61 Revisited."

> Oh, God said to Abraham, "Kill me a son"
> Abe says, "Man, you must be puttin' me on"
> God say, "No." Abe say, "What?"
> God say, "You can do what you want Abe, but
> The next time you see me comin' you better run"
> Well, Abe says, "Where do you want this killin' done?"
> God says, "Out on Highway 61."

Over the centuries, scholars have dissected, analyzed, and expounded on these verses in an attempt to explain the seemingly inexplicable. It is an *aggadic* story in which events are real but there is a hidden or allegorical meaning. Some of the language indicates the narrative may be tied to an ANE enthronement ritual.

Adonai told *Avraham*, "Now take your son, your only son, whom you love — Isaac (*Yitzchak*) — and go to the land of Moriah. Offer him there for an *olah* [burnt or raised up offering] on one of the mountains about which I will tell you" (Gen. 22.2). The term "beloved" (of which this is the first occurrence in the Bible) is synonymous with loyalty — the main attribute of an ANE covenant between a king/father and his servant/son. G-d promised *Avraham* that kings would come forth from his line, as well as from Sarah's (Gen. 17.6,15). Since *Yitzchak* was the son produced from *their* union, as heir to the throne he became "the one whom the father loved." This did not mean he was the only son in the family that the father loved, but rather he was *the* son chosen by G-d to inherit the throne. Likewise, Jacob loved Joseph more than all his other sons meaning Joseph was *the* son destined to become king. Joseph rose to be vizier in Egypt — second in command only to Pharaoh who was seen as a god.

"Your one and only" also referred to the son who would become king, and as such he would be designated the firstborn. King David was not Jesse's firstborn; but as *the* son chosen to rule, he became G-d's firstborn. In fact, David's name means "beloved." King David acknowledged *Yahweh* as his Father when he said, "You are my father, my G-d and the rock of my salvation." *Yahweh* responded, "I will set him as firstborn — the highest of the kings of earth" (Ps. 89.27,28).

> In these last days, He has spoken to us through a Son, whom He appointed heir of all things and through whom He created the universe. This Son is the radiance of His glory and the imprint of His being, upholding all things by His powerful word...For to which of the angels did God ever say, 'You are my Son. Today I have become Your Father?' And again, 'I will be to Him a Father, and He will be to me a Son?' And again, when He brings the firstborn into the world...
>
> (HEBREWS 1.2–6)

The heir to the throne became his Father's most treasured possession. *Segula* means a "peculiar treasure," which the Jewish *Targums* translate "beloved." The king's most cherished possessions included his kingdom and throne but more importantly his beloved king-son. Mesopotamian kings were called the 'peculiar treasure' of their gods. Hittite texts suggest *segula* or "beloved" refers to the special status of the new king (Quoted in Carpenter, 2009: 408n). Israel was chosen as G-d's treasured possession, His firstborn heir, to rule the nations with *Yahweh's* Covenant: the Torah (Deut. 7.6).

> If you listen closely to My voice, and keep My covenant, then you will be My own treasure from among all the people, for all the earth is Mine. So as for you, you will be to Me a kingdom of *Kohanim* and a holy nation.
>
> (EXODUS 19.5,6)

In Mesopotamia and Egypt, the monarchy was synonymous with political power. This gave rise to the concept of divine sonship. An ANE king-son was elevated to divine status through adoption. He was crowned during the annual New Year's festival and received special coronation names. The king-son was then tasked with ruling over Heaven and Earth. Israel adopted divine rulership as its official form of government. Once the king was adopted by *YHWH*, he became His divinely appointed representative on Earth and served as administrator of the government. In Israel, a special bond existed between G-d and His king — equated to a father/son relationship. This relationship may be implied when *Avraham* and *Yitzchak* "walked together as one" as they ascended the mountain of the Lord.

Adonai promised to raise up David's seed, Solomon, to build a house and establish the royal dynasty forever. "I will be a Father to him, and he will be a son to Me" (2 Sam. 7.14). David had many other sons, of course, but it was Solomon who was destined to rule the kingdom, and in so doing he became the adopted son of *Yahweh*. Adoption also meant the heir had become the "incarnation" of his father.

As incarnation or son — in any case the representative — of the (creator) deity upon the earth, the king was understood to be the earthly guarantor of the order of creation. Upon him and his acts depend the fertility of the land as well as the just social and political order of the state. Apart from this reference back to the order of creation, it is impossible to understand the numerous forms and formulations based on kingship ideology.

(SCHMIDT 1984: 105)

The enthronement of the king was linked to new birth. At his accession, the son became the only begotten of his father. "Thou art my son today, I have begotten you" was an ANE formula (found in the code of Hammurabi) for adoption. As king, David proclaimed, "I will declare the decree of *Adonai*. [*Adonai*] said to me, 'You are my son — today I have become your Father (I have begotten you). Ask of Me, and I will give you the nations as your inheritance, and the far reaches of the earth as your possession'"(7,8). Similarly, *Yahweh* spoke of *Yeshua*, "You are My Son; today I have become your Father" (Heb. 5.5).

In Psalm 110, *Yahweh* invited David to share His throne. "Your people offer themselves freely on the day you lead your host upon the holy mountains. From the womb of the morning like dew your youth will come to you" (3 RSV). Barker proposes that, "On the day you lead your host" could be translated "the day of your birth," since birth and host are similar in Hebrew. She also suggests "your youth will come to you" should be rendered "I have begotten you" (2014: 74,75).

Begotten is the Hebrew word *yalad* meaning "to be born." *Toldot*, a variation of *yalad*, means "to bear children." The first use of *toldot* refers to the union between Heaven and Earth when they were created (Gen. 2.4). Seen in a marriage context, their union produced new life — the Kingdom of Heaven was born on Earth. Adam was the firstborn of this royal dynasty to rule the kingdom. The *toldot* of Adam continued — through Seth down to Noah (Gen. 5) and Moses, from *Avraham* to King David, and to the Second Adam, *Yeshua* the Messiah.

According to Margaret Barker, establishing the Kingdom on Earth and the birth of the king-son were the same event (2014: 124). The woman in Revelation (12.1) gave birth to a son, a male child, who would rule the nations with an iron rod. This is the Davidic king (Ps. 2), whose birth was synonymous with his accession to the throne. The male child, the adopted son of the Most-High, is being presented the seat of King David. At *Yeshua's* water immersion, a voice from Heaven spoke, "You are My son, whom I love — with you I am well pleased" (Luke 3.21–22 quoted from Ps. 2.7). This is enthronement language; the beloved son is becoming king.

Adam may have had earthly parents. His "forming" from the dust could indicate a coronation event: a son being raised up from a lower level of sanctity (the dust) to become king. Adam was called *Ben Elohim* (Luke 3.38) meaning "Son of G-d." Kings in the ANE were given the title "son of god" at their enthronement. The Qumran Scrolls declare the Messiah "will be proclaimed Son of G-d; He will be called Son of G-d Most High" (4Q246). When the angel Gabriel appeared to Miriam, *Yeshua's* mother, he told her that her son would be mighty, be called *Ben Elyon* (Son of G-d), and be given the throne of David.

A king's ascent to the throne "included exaltation, anointing, becoming the Son, and ruling in judgment" (Barker 2014: 204). The king-son left the earthly realm and entered the heavenly; he was no longer the offspring of earthly parents. The new king was now the Son of his Father, G-d. The enigmatic *Melchizedek* — King of *Shalem*, *Kohen* of God Most High (Heb. 7.3) — is described as having neither beginning of days nor end of life (made like a *Ben Elohim*). *Melchizedek* was without "human" genealogy, that is, he had no earthly mother or father. Perhaps this alludes to a coronation ritual in which the king-son had been officially adopted by his Father, G-d. This may also shed light on *Yeshua's* cryptic statement, "Who is my mother? And who are my brothers?" (Matt. 12.47–50). As King and Son of G-d, *Yeshua* no longer had "earthly" mother or siblings. His family became those who would do the will of the Father to advance His kingdom.

Avraham was commended for not withholding his son. This suggests something related to *Yitzchak's* enthronement. *Avraham* was releasing his son to serve *Yahweh* as king, and *Yahweh* had become *Yitzchak's* Father.

> By myself I swear (oaths and covenants were synonymous terms) — it is a declaration of *Adonai* — because you have done this thing, and you did not withhold your son, your only son, I will richly bless you, and bountifully multiply your seed like the stars of heaven and like the sand that is on the seashore, and your seed will possess the gate of his enemies. In your seed, all the nations of the earth will be blessed — because you obeyed My voice.
>
> (GENESIS 22.15–18)

In the ANE, the gods wielded power through their kings. The king's duty was to maintain and uphold the created order, and so the king-son became the channel through whom prosperity and fertility flowed to the people. A benevolent king ensured the kingdom flourished; he secured material and spiritual blessings, lifted up the poor, and protected the oppressed from foreign domination. As impartial judge, he governed over the economic, judicial, social, and moral affairs of the kingdom so the kingdom did not descend into chaos.

In short, ancient Near Eastern cosmic, political, and social order find their unity under the concept of "creation." Only from this background it is possible to understand why in the whole ancient Near east, including Israel, an offense in the legal realm obviously has effects in the realm of nature (drought, famine) or in the political sphere (threat of the enemy). Law, nature, and politics are only aspects of one comprehensive order of creation. This comprehensive character and its fundamental appreciation of the order of creation found vivid expression in the kingship ideology of the ancient Near east.

(SCHMIDT 1984: 105)

According to N.T. Wright, the first-century people understood that the world worked best when ruled by a wise steward who was humble before G-d. This allowed the king to bring order to the world and to be accountable for the power he was given. "G-d wanted his world ordered under the rule of humans — but it didn't mean everything human rulers did was right. It meant human rulers were answerable to God" (2012: 169) who was the supreme judge over the affairs of men.

One of most quoted verses from the New Testament contains enthronement language:

> For G-d so *loved the world*, that he gave his *one and only Son*, that whoever believes in him should not perish, but have eternal life…He who believes in him is not condemned. He who does not believe has been condemned already, because he has not believed in the name of the *one and only Son of G-d*.

(JOHN 3.16,17)

The "one and only" is *Yahweh's* adopted king-son, *Yeshua* the Messiah, who suffered and died on a tree in order to restore the Kingdom of Heaven on Earth. He overcame death to bring deliverance (salvation) for those enslaved by the world's tyrants — the beasts and monsters in the field. *Yeshua* judged his Father's enemies — setting free those enchained to the kingdoms of this world. "Once you lose the kingdom theme which is central to the gospels everything is re-interpreted in ways that substitute a different gospel message" (Wright 2012: 158). Wright adds that this verse has been interpreted in the context of personal salvation but, in reality, is addressing G-d's rulership over the whole earth.

The Anointed One

Thy word is a lamp unto my feet and a light unto my path.
(PSALM 119.105)

Coronation rituals in the ancient world transformed the servant/son from human being to divine king. In Egypt, the enthronement ceremony formally elevated the king's legal status to that of a god. The Isaiah scroll (52.14) from Qumran alludes to this. Barker suggests the text in Isaiah should not have been translated "the one marred (*mashchat*) beyond human resemblance" but rather "the one anointed (*maschach*) who no longer looked like an ordinary human being" (2000: 6). "The heavenly and earthly identity of Jacob, the Man who slept at *Beit El* (house of G-d) was at the same time an image on the throne in heaven" (Gen. *Rabbah* 68.12). Origen (Greek scholar and early Christian theologian) explained that the *Prayer of Joseph*, a Jewish text, reveals something similar: "Both a man on earth and an angel in heaven, I, Jacob who am speaking to you, am also Israel, an angel of G-d, and a ruling spirit" (quoted in Barker 2014: 129). Jacob/Israel, the servant, was transformed at *Beit El* to become the nation's ruler under the sovereignty of G-d. Paul describes *Yeshua* as the divine Son of G-d, the King of Kings, who is, "the image of the invisible G-d" and "the firstborn of creation."

For by Him all things were created — in heaven and on earth, the seen and the unseen, whether thrones or angelic powers or rulers or authorities. All was created through

Him and for Him. He exists before everything, and in Him all holds together. He is the head of the body, His community. He is the beginning, the firstborn from the dead. For G-d was pleased to have all His fullness dwell in Him.

(COL. 1.15–20)

At the transfiguration, *Yeshua's* form was changed; his face shone like the sun, his clothes became white as the light, and he was overshadowed by a bright cloud — meaning the Presence of G-d anointed him as king. With his royal status confirmed, the Father declared, "This is My Son, whom I love; with Him I am will pleased" (Matt 17.5). The transfiguration took place on the seventh day on a high mountain which is a symbol for a temple. The seven days of creation are a pattern for enthronement. G-d rested (took the throne) on the seventh day; His Presence entered His Cosmic Temple in order to rule. "The seven days are not given as the period of time over which the material cosmos came into existence, but the period of time devoted to the inauguration of the functions of the cosmic temple" (Walton 2009: 91).

In ancient Israel, an enthronement took place in stages. The first phase consisted of presenting the royal insignia, anointing with oil, and receiving the acclamation of the people. In the second stage, the king took his seat on the throne and was paid homage by court officials (De Vaux 1961: 102). Solomon rode his father's mule down to the Gihon Spring for the first stage of his coronation. The donkey was the traditional mount of honor, so to ride King David's mule was to claim the throne. *Zadok*, the priest, poured anointing oil from a ram's horn onto Solomon's head — to form a wreath. As the shofar sounded, the crowd roared, "Long live King Solomon!" (I Kings 1:38–39). This confirmed that the people had accepted *Yahweh's* choice as king. Then Solomon ascended the mountain to take his seat on the throne.

Six days before Passover, *Yeshua* traveled to Bethany (located on the Mount of Olives) to the home of Lazarus whom *Yeshua* had raised from the dead. Miriam anointed his feet with oil and dried them with her hair; the fragrance from the perfumed oil filled their house. In Mark and Matthew's account, a woman pours expensive oil over *Yeshua's* head at the home of Simon the Leper (Mark 14.3, Matt. 26.7). In ancient Mesopotamia and Assyria, bathing with perfumed oil was a purification rite belonging solely to the gods, royal families, and high officials. Oil was used for cleansing the feet of the god (Feliu 2003: 104).

This anointing with oil was a ritual act in preparation for his burial as well as his accession to the throne. The following day, as *Yeshua* entered the city, many people lined the road to Jerusalem waving palm branches. They spread their clothes before him and shouted in acclamation, "Hosanna to the Son of David! Blessed is He who comes in the name of the Lord!" By riding a donkey into Jerusalem, *Yeshua* was claiming the throne. On the seventh day, Passover, he was crucified. Resurrected from the dead, the king ushered in a new kingdom that would fill the earth through his image-bearers.

The oil used for anointing Israel's kings and priests came from the olive tree. The seven-branched *menorah* was compared to an *etz shemen*: an oil tree. In Mesopotamia, the deity's heavenly dwelling was represented by the temple grove. Its sacred tree was the king — the deity's Gardener "who was anointed with oil of the sacred tree, crowned with a wreath of its leaves and blossoms, and had a rod or scepter of its branches" (Widengren 1951: 42).

Enoch characterized the *menorah* as the Tree of Life, which according to the *Apocalypse of Moses* (9) was an olive tree whose oil was a great light and whose anointing was excellent (*Legends of the Jews*, Vol. 5). David called himself a green olive tree in the House of G-d (Ps. 52:8). In Zechariah's vision, two olive trees were standing on either side of a *menorah*. Extending from their branches were two golden pipes out of which oil was poured into the *menorah's* bowls. Zechariah identified the "two olives trees" as *Yehoshua*, the high priest, and *Zerubabbel*, the prince who served as ruler over the nation. Called the sons of oil, these two stood as the anointed ones who would rebuild the Temple (Zech. 4:1–14) so that the Presence of G-d could return.

Descriptions of the *menorah* (Ex. 25.31–40; 37.17–24) liken it to a tree with branches that extend from a central shaft. Philo's writings suggest the *menorah* was the "Tree of Life" in the garden sanctuary (*Questions on Genesis* 1.10). Enoch saw a gold, fiery tree in the garden that he also identified as the Tree of Life (2 Enoch 8.3,4). In the ANE, the trunk of a tree of life was the ritual symbol for both the god and his king (Widengren 1951: 42). Philo said the central shaft of the *menorah* represented the king who was an angelic being in the heavenly Tabernacle just as the high priest was in the earthly Temple (Heir 215, 216).

Barker said the *menorah* was equally the Presence of G-d with his people and *the* symbol for the dynasty. Clement of Alexandria concluded *Yeshua* was the *menorah* linked to the royal tree (*Stromata* v.6). Finally, the *Targum on Genesis* (Jonathan) suggests the *Etz Chaim*, the Tree of Life, was the Torah filled with fruit that nourished the just who were like trees planted in water. The lampstand was a stylized tree going back to the Tree of Life in the garden. It was a reflection of the Presence of G-d, and in the Temple it stood at the cosmic center of the universe (Meyers 1985: 546).

Proverbs (3:18) links Wisdom to a Tree of Life whose fruit gives wisdom, whose leaves provide healing, and whose oil opens blind eyes. King Solomon was endowed with wisdom upon his coronation. "Wisdom that surpassed the wisdom of all the sons of the east and all the wisdom of Egypt" (I Kings 5.10). Anointing the king's head with oil symbolized wisdom being poured into his mind. Paul exhorted the Romans to be "transformed by the renewing of the mind" and not conformed to the thinking of the world (Rom. 12.2). The anointing oil was the Spirit renewing the mind — providing godly wisdom to G-d's priests and kings.

Temple priests serviced the *menorah* each day: They filled the bowls with pure olive oil, trimmed and/or replaced the wicks, and rekindled the lights so the lamps would burn throughout the night. The oil was tied to the new king's renewal of the kingdom. The *menorah* became a symbol for the spiritual and physical light that radiated out to the people from G-d's House. Some scholars have seen a connection between Aaron tending the lampstand in the Tabernacle and G-d's creation of light on the first day. The high priest represented the Creator as he serviced the *menorah* in the evenings and in the mornings. Both the Temple and the city of Jerusalem were called "the light of the world" (Genesis *Rabbah* 59). *Yeshua* described his Kingdom of Priests as the light of the world. He compared them to a city set on hill that cannot be hidden and to a lamp in a lampstand that gives light to everyone in the House (Matt. 5.14,15).

At the king's anointing, the oil was poured from a ram's horn. A ram symbolized leadership and authority; its horns denoted strength and power. "By my Name [*Yahweh*] his horn [King David] will be exalted" (Ps. 89.25). Hannah's son, Samuel (prophet and priest) was described as a horn lifted high. *Adonai* exalted the horn of His anointed one when Samuel became ruler over Israel (I Sam. 2.10). At *Rosh HaShanah* (New Year in the ancient world), a *shofar* (trumpet) made from a ram's horn was blown as part of the king's coronation. In the *Akeidah*, a ram was caught in a thicket by his horns; it became the substitute offering for *Yitzchak*. According to the book of Enoch, both David and Solomon were sheep before their accession. Then they were transformed into rams once they were enthroned (I Enoch 89.45,48).

In the Septuagint, *arnion* is translated "lamb," but it can also mean a young ram. Revelation's throne room scene (5) pictures a lamb/ram with seven horns and seven eyes — the seven spirits of G-d sent out into all the earth. The seven spirits speak of the anointed king who is the Lion of the Tribe of Judah, the Root of David, and the only one worthy to open the scroll. The lamb/ram is raised up as king to shepherd his people, and he leads them to fountains of living water (Gihon Spring). A multitude from every nation stands before the throne and before the lamb/ram. Clothed in white robes holding palm branches, they cry out in acclamation, "Salvation belongs to our G-d, who sits on the throne, and to the Ram" (Rev. 7.9).

Many of the significant events in *Yeshua's* life are tied to enthronement. At his conception, an angel told his mother, Miriam, that the *Ruach HaKodesh* (spirit) would overshadow her — symbolizing the anointing by the Presence of G-d. At *Yeshua's* birth, he was called *Ben Elohim*, Son of G-d (Luke 1.35), and magi from the east came looking for the One who was born King of the Jews (Matt. 1.2). At his water immersion, the heavens opened and the Spirit of the Lord descended like a dove. His kingship was confirmed when the voice of G-d declared, "You are My Son whom I love" (Luke 3.22). At *Yeshua's* transfiguration, a cloud overshadowed him, and a voice again confirmed his rulership, saying, "This is my Son whom I love" (Matt 17.5). Sitting on the Mount of Olives, overlooking the Temple, *Yeshua* shared with his disciples the "sign" of his coming; he said they would see the Son of Man coming in a cloud with power and great glory — filled with the Presence of G-d (Matt 24). Upon entering Jerusalem before his crucifixion, *Yeshua* received the acclamation of the people; they waved palm branches acknowledging *Yeshua* as their king (Jn. 12.13). Some watched as *Yeshua* was taken up, and a cloud, that is the Presence of G-d, received him (Acts 1.9). In the transfiguration (Luke 9.31), Moses and Elijah spoke of this "departure" as *the* Exodus (Luke 9.31). In Revelation

(5), the twenty-four elders, the heavenly court's royal officials, paid homage to the king as they fell down and worshipped the lamb/ram. The Messiah was seated on the throne ruling over his Kingdom.

✡   ✡   ✡

The following *midrashic* story is loosely based on the narrative in the first chapter of the Gospel of John — a chapter that follows the pattern of the creation week.

Elohim pushed back the waters of chaos. When dry ground appeared, He took His eternal seed from a pure gold rectangular box and prepared it for His garden. The master gardener worked the soil, planted the seed, and watered His treasure until it sprouted. The seed produced the Word of G-d. It grew into a mighty Tree of Life whose majestic trunk supported a glorious canopy that spanned the expanse of the heavens. Its branches swelled as though filled with pure olive oil. The skies were ablaze; thick smoke enveloped the heavenly chamber. A brilliant light illuminated the hidden corners of the lower world and exposed the works of darkness. The Tree of Life was *the* true light that came into the world — a world that refused to recognize *Elohim's* sovereignty. The Word was named *Ben Elohim*, Son of G-d — a coronation title. *Elohim* fashioned a House on Earth for his Son then placed a solid gold throne — adorned with emeralds, turquoise, and carnelian — to the right of *His* throne.

The Word put on a *ketonet* (tunic) of skins and became *the* visible image-bearer and incarnation of his Father. A living Tabernacle filled with *Elohim's* Presence, he was sent into the field to repair the broken covenant — to remove the curse called death that intruded on life. The field was a domain lacking in life-giving water; briars and thistles sprang up and dominated the landscape. The Word of G-d worked the ground and, like other men, was subjected to the many hardships of life in the field. Unlike other men, he never broke covenant with his Father. Therefore, he enjoyed *Elohim's* divine protection.

The Word arrived in the Galilee, the lower circuit between Heaven and Earth. It was a garden paradise with rich soil that produced an abundance of fruit from the local trees: walnut, palm, olive, and fig. The Son of G-d invited Philip to become an attendant in his Kingdom. Then he saw Philip's friend, Nathaniel, resting under the canopy of a towering fig tree — *the* symbol of the Kings of Judah. The Word declared Nathaniel a beacon of truth. Nathaniel proclaimed his allegiance to *Elohim's* Son, the King of Israel. Soon, they would see Heaven opened and angels ascending and descending on the Son of Man.

In time, the royal seed would suffer a tortuous death at the hands of Earth's cruel tyrants. But the Word would rise again, overcome *Elohim's* enemies, and take his seat at the right hand of his Father. As the Son hung on the tree, in unimaginable pain and agony, he ushered in *Elohim's* glorious Kingdom. On that tree, at the center of creation where Heaven and Earth meet, the Word of G-d broke the back of human power. The Word smashed the nations with his iron scepter and dashed to pieces their corrupt empires. He removed the curse, set his covenant people free, and delivered his subjects from the long night of oppression caused by those who conspired against *YHWH*.

At the Son's resurrection, Heaven's firmament split and the Word returned to his Father's House. He left behind the *Elohim's Ruach* for His covenant people so they could rule the earth in Wisdom as His kings and priests. *Elohim's* Kingdom advanced in secret; it broke through enemy strongholds, deploying the kingdom's most powerful weapon: TRUTH. Truth to illuminate the plethora of lies told by the world's tyrants. Truth to rightly judge their monstrous deeds. Truth that set free the suffering, the broken, and the hurting. Truth that brought healing, forgiveness of sin, and renewed fellowship with G-d for those living in the field. Slowly but surely, the kingdom multiplied and spread and filled the entire earth. Even though the Son spread his precious seed in harsh, uncultivated soil, it still sprouted and produced exquisite, flowering trees and shrubs; his luscious fruit-bearing trees continually replaced the field's thorns and thistles.

After the Word rose from the dead, he returned to the Galilee to the mountain where he had arranged to meet his disciples. He confirmed that he was given all authority in Heaven and on Earth and that he would be with them until the end of the age — when Heaven and Earth finally re-united and the garden returned.

One Day, called a Jubilee, Creation's Temple was restored to its original state. The anointed king came riding on his white stallion, on the wings of a cloud, passing through Heaven's portal. His blood-red robes still displayed the stains of his crucifixion. Accompanying him was Heaven's priestly army, angel-like servants clothed in fine white linen garments, also riding white horses. The Word took his seat on Earth's throne, *Elohim's* holy mountain, *Tziyon* (Zion), the garden paradise, and began to rule in the Spirit of righteousness and justice.

> For as the heavens are higher than earth, so are My ways higher than your ways, and My thoughts than your thoughts. For as the rain and snow come down from heaven, and do not return there without having watered the earth, making it bring forth and sprout, giving seed to sow and bread to eat, so My word will be that goes out from My mouth. It will not return to Me in vain, but will accomplish what I intend, and will succeed in what I sent it for.
>
> (ISAIAH 55.9–11)

Mount of Anointment

The Mount of Olives is the location for a number of events in the Bible. It's also called the Mount of Anointment, so named for its many olive groves. The oil produced from the fruit of the trees was used to kindle the *menorah* in the Temple and to anoint Israel's kings and priests. Symbolically, the oil was G-d's Presence resting on His kings and filling His House. The Mount of Olives may have been the location for the *Akeidah* (the binding of *Yitzchak*) when *Avraham* declared, "On this mountain the Lord will be seen." Perhaps this was an allusion to the oil produced from the olive trees that gave Wisdom (sight) to His kings.

Part of a mountain range on the eastern side of the Old City of Jerusalem, the Mount consists of three peaks: The Mount of Olives in the center, Mount Scopus on the North, and the Mount of Corruption on the South, which was named for the idol worship promulgated by King Solomon (I Kings 11.7–8). Formed mostly from sedimentary rock, the mountain is composed of a soft, chalky substance that is not good for construction. Therefore, beginning in the time of the First Temple, instead of being a place for homes and villages, the mountain became a place to bury the dead.

Absalom, King David's son, attempted to set himself up as ruler of Judah forcing his father to leave Jerusalem. David reluctantly ascended the northern path of the Mount — barefoot and weeping with his head covered (2 Sam. 15.30). The legitimate king headed east as if being sent into exile. This was a familiar pattern. Adam was exiled from the garden and moved east into the field. Judah was forced out of the land of Israel, exiled to the east in Babylon, by King Nebuchadnezzar.

Near the summit of the Mount of Olives, a special ceremony marking the start of *Rosh Chodesh* (new or head of the month) was held. According to the *Mishnah*, "The ascent to the *Rosh*" (head) went up the mountain of the olive, which was also called the mountain of *maschiach* (messiah). Following the court's official confirmation of the sighting of the new moon, a relay system was set in place to communicate to the rest of the nation. Standing on the *Rosh*, a priest lit a signal fire using oil wood, then waved the burning pole from side to side and up and down (*Rosh haShanah* 2.3,4). From the adjacent mountain, someone would repeat the process. The fires that started at the Mount of Anointment were first seen at Sarteba, a prominent hill in Samaria, then at *Beit Biotin* "where a signal fire was waved until a man could see the whole exile before him like a sea of fire" (2.2).

The *Rosh* was also the location for the red heifer offering. A three-year-old heifer was chosen: entirely red, without any blemish, and one that had never been yoked. After the animal was completely consumed, its ashes were mixed with water and sprinkled on the priests for purification from corpse uncleanness. The ceremony removed any defilement caused by contact with the dead (those defiled were impure for seven days). The *Rosh* was designated a "clean" place outside the camp of Israel. A procession of priests, led by the high priest, came through the East Gate of the Temple and crossed the Kidron Valley over a special bridge that was aligned with the entrance of the sanctuary. There was a *mikvah* (immersion bath) at the *Rosh* for the high priest to immerse if he chose to perform the task of purification. A vessel was filled with water flowing from a natural source, then the ashes from the heifer were added. After sunrise on the third day and seventh day, the mixture was sprinkled on the body of the one in need of purification. Symbolically, the offering of the red heifer was related to repentance.

Key events in *Yeshua's* life took place on the Mount of Olives: His triumphal entry into Jerusalem, his betrayal and arrest, his resurrection and ascension, and some scholars have suggested the Mount was the site of his crucifixion. In the first century, a northern path (called the ascent), led up to the summit. A southern route (called the descent) connected to Bethany and Bethphage — two places *Yeshua* often visited. Bethphage was within the Sabbatical limit of Jerusalem (the distance that can be walked on the Sabbath) and was home to the priests responsible for maintaining the *Rosh*. Bethphage means House of Unripe Figs — perhaps also an indictment on the spiritual condition of Israel's leadership. Jeremiah described them as bad fruit (Jer. 24.8); they were trees that produced only green, immature, and unpalatable figs. The fig tree was a symbol for Israel's kings.

By contrast Bethany, or possibly *Beit Tehna* in Hebrew, means House of Ripe Figs and was located on the south-eastern slope of the Mount of Olives. Home to Lazarus, whom *Yeshua* raised from the dead, and to Miriam, who anointed *Yeshua* with oil, Bethany was where *Yeshua* led his disciples after he appeared to them in Jerusalem following his resurrection. "And while blessing them, he departed from them, and was taken up into heaven" (Luke 24.51). "The disciples worshipped *Yeshua*, as Messiah, then they returned to Jerusalem in great joy and continued praising in the Temple" (52,53).

On "Palm Sunday," *Yeshua* rode a donkey down the southern path from nearby Bethany. The crowds hailed him as the Messianic Son of David — the rightful king. During the last week of his life, *Yeshua* ascended and descended the Mount of Olives many times — taking the southern path down to the city and the Temple in the mornings and walking up the ascent in the evenings back to Bethany.

With his disciples, *Yeshua* also frequented the Garden of Gethsemane (Jn. 18.2) which was located on the western slope of the Mount of Olives across the Kidron Valley from Jerusalem. Gethsemane (*Gat shemen*) is generally translated "oil press" for the pressing of the olives. However, *gat* likely means a wine press. In the Septuagint, *gat* (I Sam. 6.17) is the trough where the grapes were trodden with the feet. In the garden, on the night before his crucifixion, *Yeshua's* disciples fell asleep as he prayed nearby. About to be betrayed by Judas, exhausted from grief and in great anguish, *Yeshua* sweat drops of blood that fell to the ground (Luke 22:39–40). A picture emerges of grapes being squeezed in the wine press — a symbol for a crucible of suffering.

I [*Adonai*] have trodden the winepress alone — from the peoples, no man was with Me. I trod them in My anger, and trampled them in My wrath. Their lifeblood spattered My garments, so I stained all My robes...so I trod down the peoples, in My anger, and made them drunk in My wrath, and I poured out their lifeblood on the earth.

(ISAIAH 63.3,6)

To produce oil, olives were beaten and squeezed in an oil press. Pressure was required to bring forth the oil. "The children of Israel were to bring pure olive oil beaten for the light to cause the lamp to burn always" (Ex. 27.20). The olive oil used in the *menorah* was made by smashing the olives by hand and then allowing the oil to drip for several days. The rabbis compared a man to the olive who must be beaten and bruised in order to glow with light. Rabbi Weiss said, "It appears the olive is destroyed, but what is actually happening is the bitterness is being removed and the oil, the sweetness, is being saved and purified to send light into the world." *Yeshua*, the servant king who represented Israel and who bore our griefs, carried our pains, and was crushed because of our iniquities, became the light of the world.

The Olivet Discourse also took place on the Mount of Olives. Perhaps *Yeshua* sat with his disciples near the summit at the altar of the red heifer where the signal fires were set. Gazing across the Kidron valley towards the west, they could see into the Temple precincts. "All the [Temple] walls were high, save only the eastern wall, because the priest that burns the Heifer and stands on top of the Mount of Olives should be able to look directly into the entrance of the sanctuary when the blood [of the Red Heifer] is sprinkled" (*Kodeshim*: Mishnah *Middoth* 2:4). The disciples asked *Yeshua* for the sign of his coming and the end of the age. He answered by describing the coming destruction of the Temple and the persecution of his people (Matt 24, Luke 21, Mark 13). The sign that would appear in the heavens was the Temple. At his resurrection, which was the launching of the new creation, *Yeshua* became *the* new creation Temple filled with the Presence of G-d; his disciples, his image-bearers, could now follow and spread the message of the Kingdom around the world through love.

Finally, it was on the Mount of Olives, likely at the *Rosh*, that *Yeshua* was taken up and received in a cloud. As his disciples were staring into heaven, two men wearing white clothing appeared to them and said, "In the same way you saw him leave, he will return" (Acts 1.9–11). This confirms what Ezekiel had prophesied, that in the same way the glory left the Temple and the city and moved to the mountain east of the city, so too the glory would return from the east mountain to the House (43.1). The arrival of the cloud, symbolic of the Presence of G-d, signaled to those living in the land of Israel (who were experiencing a type of exile under Rome, Herod Antipas, and a corrupt Temple leadership) that their long night of exile was over. *Yeshua* brought redemption to the nation; he reclaimed the people's freedom and cleared their debts by paying with his life. In the context of the first century, paying a ransom meant securing the freedom of a slave from the slave market.

It was *Chag haMatzah*, the Feast of Unleavened Bread, when he took the cup, gave thanks, and offered his disciples to drink, saying, "For this is my blood of the covenant, which is poured out for many for the removal of sins" (Matt 26.28). The Greek word for remission or removal of sins is *aphesis*, which is *Yovel* in Hebrew. The *Yovel* (50th year) marked the release from debts and a return of property to its original owner. The blood of the new covenant being poured out signaled a release from sin's grasp. (It will be "That Day," a *Yom Echad*, when *Yeshua* will drink anew with his disciples in his Father's kingdom.) After singing a hymn, they went out to the Mount of Olives, to Gethsemane, where he would ultimately be arrested.

On That Day, his feet will stand on the Mount of Olives, east of Jerusalem, and the Mount of Olives will be split in two from east to west, forming a great valley, with half of the mountain moving north and half moving south.

(ZECHARIAH 14.4)

The earth splitting represented "the chaos between [the fall of] one kingdom and [the rise of] another" (Beale and Carson 2007: 1105). A splitting (*bakah*) separated two kingdoms: the kingdoms of this world and the Kingdom of Heaven. The rise of a new Kingdom out of the chaos of the old meant G-d's House was being rebuilt and restored to Israel. The foundations of the earth split after Noah and his family entered the ark — rescued from the violence of the age. Moses split the sea allowing Israel to be delivered from Pharaoh. He also split the rock in the wilderness camp providing the people with life-giving water. At Solomon's enthronement ceremony, the earth split (I Kings 1.40) as the people rejoiced over their new king. The curtain in the Temple split as *Yeshua* hung on the tree — indicating a new Kingdom was rising up to replace the old order. "The coming of Jesus represented the manifestation of a primordial, world-shattering force that produced a deep rupture in the very fabric of reality itself" (Ulansey 2016: *Heavens Torn Open*).

And behold the curtain of the Temple was split in two, from top to bottom. And the earth quaked and rocks were split apart. And the tombs were opened, and many bodies of the *kedoshim* (saints) who were sleeping were raised to life. And coming forth out of the tombs after His resurrection, they went into the holy city and appeared to many. Now the centurion and those with him keeping guard over *Yeshua* when they saw the earthquake and what was happening, they became terribly frightened and said, this really was the Son of G-d.

(MATTHEW 27.51–54)

Yeshua's tomb was made secure. It was sealed at the entrance with a stone while a soldier stood guard. After the *Shabbat*, at dawn on the first day of the week (an eighth day), the two *Miriams* arrived at the tomb when suddenly there was a great earthquake. (Miriam of Magdala believes *Yeshua* is the gardener/king) An Angel of the Lord descended from Heaven and rolled back the stone and sat on it. The Angel then told the women that the tomb was empty and *Yeshua* had risen from the dead.

He was now *the* raised-up sukkah of his father, King David; he was the new creation Temple, and the new Jerusalem — the place where the Presence of G-d dwelled. In him, Heaven and Earth met, and mankind had access to G-d. NT Wright explains that a new creation had begun, and a new people had been formed in the power of the spirit as they were being resurrected from the grave (2012: 79). The *kedoshim* (set apart ones) came to life, reborn as kings and priests, when their tombs on the Mount of Olives split open. The splitting of the sea, the earth, the veil, and the tombs were the sign that the way to the garden was open and no barrier existed between the people and the throne of G-d. The whole earth would become a temple to YHWH and his priests and kings restored to His image.

The Kingdom was being restored back to its original owner, and the breach in the broken creation covenant was in the process of being repaired. His image-bearers would finish the work.

> I saw no Temple in her, for its Temple is *Adonai Elohei Tzva'ot* and the Lamb. And the city has no need for the sun or the moon to shine on it, for the glory of G-d lights it up, and its lamp is the Lamb. The nations shall walk by its light, and the kings of the earth bring their glory into it. Its gates shall never be shut by day, for there shall be no night there! And they shall bring into it the glory and honor of the nations.
>
> (REVELATION 21.22–26)

CHAPTER FIVE

PRIESTS

But you are a chosen people, a royal priesthood,
a holy nation, a people for G-d's own possession,
so that you may proclaim the praises of the One who
called you out of darkness into His marvelous light.
Honor all people. Love the brotherhood.
Fear G-d. Honor the King.
(I Peter 2.9,17)

G-d established a covenant with the heavens and the earth. Called a *Brit Esh* (covenant of fire), His Word/oath manifested as tongues of fire. "The voice of G-d hews out flames of fire" (Ps. 29.7). His Presence appeared as a consuming blaze in "This World" and as a purifying fire in the "World to Come." Enoch called G-d's inner chamber, which housed His oracle, the "House of the Tongues of Fire." It was there His glory, seated on the throne, resembled rivers of flaming fire as it streamed from above and below the heavenly chamber (I Enoch 14).

At the conclusion of the creation week, G-d inaugurated His Kingdom in a garden. He placed Adam, His king-priest and image-bearer, inside the sanctuary to cultivate the soil, guard the sacred space, and serve as mediator between Heaven and Earth. After disobeying the terms of the covenant, Adam was exiled from the garden into the field. His service, however, was not changed; the command given him, to expand G-d's Presence throughout the earth and to prepare mankind to receive the sovereign rule of G-d, was not rescinded.

After the exodus from Egypt, the Kingdom was inaugurated on Sinai's mountain. At the foot of the mountain, a newly formed nation, Israel, witnessed a betrothal ceremony between the heavens and the earth. The mountain shook violently. The sound of thunder and the blast of a shofar announced the new Kingdom — risen from the chaos of the old in Egypt. G-d gave Moses, His king-priest, the blueprints for building the Tabernacle based on the pattern of His Cosmic House. In the desert wilderness, His Presence would dwell in the midst of Israel as fire in a thick cloud before the people. Israel, now called a Kingdom of Priests and a holy nation, was tasked with mediating between Heaven and Earth — serving in the Tabernacle, which was the bridge between G-d and the surrounding nations. G-d presented His Word/oath to Moses on tablets of stone.

At *Yeshua's* crucifixion, the Kingdom was inaugurated on a tree, and the role of king and high priest was restored in the Second Adam. "...Messiah appeared as *Kohen Gadol* (high priest) of the good things that have now come passing through the greater and more perfect Tent not made with hands (that is to say not of this creation)" (Heb. 9.11). The curtain in the Temple split, the earth quaked, rocks split apart, and tombs were opened — proving the Kingdom of Heaven had broken through from the world beyond time. Heaven and Earth united in his resurrected body — now *the* new creation Temple which houses the Presence of G-d. "But if the Temple was always the sign and the means of the true theocracy, then the Temple-in-person, that is, Jesus himself is now that sign. The one who sits in heaven is the one who rules on earth" (Wright 2012: 247). For the messiah is the one who "makes creation a cosmos instead of a chaos" (Lightfoot 1977: 156). *Yeshua's* followers, his loyal attendants, were charged with spreading the sovereignty of G-d throughout the world, which they did by forming communities that operated under the power of G-d.

At *Shavuot* (Pentecost, Feast of Weeks), tongues of fire appeared and settled on those sitting in the Temple (Acts 2.1–3). As *Yeshua* had promised at his resurrection, they were filled with the Divine Presence. Those who came to celebrate at the Temple, from "every nation under heaven," heard, in their own language, the mighty deeds of G-d. The Word/oath of G-d, that had once been written on tablets of stone, was being written on human hearts.

G-d promised Israel He would gather the *goyim* (nations) to see His glory and elevate them as priests and Levites (Is. 66.21). With the launching of His Kingdom, G-d offered the Gentiles a place to serve in His Cosmic House. "The reason that God will 'take' Gentiles for priests and for Levites is because now the place of true worship and temple service is not geographically located in the old, temporal Jerusalem, but throughout the entire earth, where all mankind will come to bow down before [Him] forever" (Beale 2004: 137°138). This is the sign in the heavens: G-d's Presence dwells in the midst of His new creation temple — those who are in covenant with Him.

Together, Adam and *Chavah* resembled a miniature cosmic temple, and the fruit borne from their union numbered the stars in the heavens. Adam made a covenant with the earth that ensured blessings on the fruit the ground produced. Eating, considered the highest form of worship in the Temple, was part of his covenantal obligation. "To take and to eat" was likened to the stages of ancient marriage covenants: the betrothal followed by the wedding ceremony; both rituals were accompanied by a meal. In ANE covenants, only parties who were at peace could dine together. Sharing a meal meant breaking bread and drinking wine, which ratified the agreement the parties were making. After *Yeshua's* resurrection, his covenant community devoted themselves to fellowship, prayer, and breaking bread. *Yeshua* has promised he will drink the fruit of the vine, anew, with those in his Father's Kingdom (Matt. 26.29).

When Adam and *Chavah* ate from the Tree of Knowledge of Good and Evil, they "joined" themselves to that which was forbidden: comparable to physical adultery. Israel often formed unauthorized alliances with foreign kings that included worshipping their gods. By doing so, Israel repeatedly became the harlot. The Torah provides boundaries that would have protected Israel from committing idolatry, but she often ignored its counsel. When Moses was about to die, *Adonai* gave him this warning: "[Then] this people will rise up and prostitute themselves with foreign gods of the land they are entering. They will abandon Me and break My covenant that I cut with them" (Deut. 31.16). God told the prophet Hosea to marry a harlot (Gomer) who was a picture of adulterous Israel. "For the land is an unfaithful prostitute, far from following after *Adonai*" (Hosea 1.2). In the book of Revelation, Israel's temple leadership is described as the great prostitute, who sits on many waters, with whom the kings of the earth commit sexual immorality. "Those who dwell on the earth got drunk with the wine of her immorality" (17.2b). G-d promised that His anger would flare up against them and that His tongue, a flaming fire, would devour them in a jealous rage.

Therefore, harlot, hear the word of *Adonai*! Because your filth was poured out and your nakedness exposed through your harlotry with your lovers, because of all the idols of your abominations, and because of the blood of your children that you gave them, I will gather all your lovers — those you have pleased and all those you have loved, with all them that you have hated…I will judge you, as women who commit adultery… Then I will bring on you the blood of fury and jealousy…I will give you into their hand…they will set your houses on fire and execute judgment on you in the sight of many women. So, I will cause you to stop your harlotry.

(EZEKIEL 16.35–38,41)

Israel played the harlot with the Assyrians, and Judah with the Babylonians (Ezek. 23). Described as depraved sisters lusting after men in uniform, they both reaped the consequences of their adultery — exile — which meant G-d's Presence was removed from their midst. Moved by a spirit of jealousy, G-d handed them over to foreign kings who enslaved them. Nations rose up against them — sending armed soldiers riding chariots to slaughter their sons and daughters with the sword and to destroy their cities by burning them to the ground. In the first century, with tacit approval from the Temple leadership, the high priest aligned with Rome. In Revelation, the high priest (like the city of Jerusalem) was clothed in purple and scarlet (his regular garments were woven of purple, scarlet, blue and white linen), was adorned with gold and precious stones (Rev. 17.4; 18.16), and was called the great harlot who corrupted the earth and the one who shed the blood of G-d's servants (Rev. 19.2).

In the garden, the ramifications for breaking the covenant fell on the defiled parties: *Adam*, the *adamah* (ground), *Chavah*, and the serpent. In the ancient world, being *cursed* simply meant the guilty reaped the consequences; the hedge of protection that the covenant provided was removed by the offending party's lack of fealty. In this case, the consequence for eating fruit from the Tree of Knowledge was death. Death, however, did not mean the *end* of life. Death was an enemy who entered in through a breach in the covenant, disrupted the *Shalem*, and created chaos inside the house. This can be compared to an ANE king whose army breached the city walls — captured, killed, or displaced its residents — and left the city desolate.

Death can also be defined as exile from the camp and separation from the Presence of G-d. "How fortunate are those who wash their robes, so that they may have the right to the Tree of Life and may enter through the gates into the city. Outside are the dogs, and the sorcerers and the sexually immoral and the murderers and the idolaters, and everyone who loves and practices falsehood" (Rev. 22. 14, 15). When the Divine Presence tabernacled with us in *Yeshua* the Messiah, who was G-d's new creation Temple raised up from the earth, eternal life became a guarantee. Death was simply a momentary intrusion on life.

Adam and *Chavah's* disobedience caused their "relationship" with the ground to become strained. The man and woman trusted in themselves to build a kingdom instead of trusting in their creator. Once they were removed from the garden, the sacred space could heal and be set free from its contamination. *Yahweh* graciously upheld the mandate given mankind to work the soil and bring forth fruit — even in exile. The ground, however, had also borne the consequences of the man's actions. Growing food in soil that yielded thorns and thistles would prove challenging. Sustaining life in the field meant toil, sweat, and heartbreak.

The woman also faced the consequences of her actions: She would know sorrow in conception and endure pain in childbirth. Her longing would be for her *eish* (man or husband). In this context, "man" is plural; this may be referring to humanity in general. Perhaps this indicates her desire to reproduce the beast-like nature of human beings rather than the nature of G-d. The man would *mashal* (dominion, rule) over *Chavah*, meaning he would exercise dominion through "human will" in order to push back the chaos he had created. The word *mashal* is first used in the creation week. The greater light "ruled" the day, the lesser light "ruled" the night, and the stars "ruled" over the day and night (Gen. 1.16). This explains Joseph's dream in which his father (Jacob) was compared to the sun, his mother (Rachel) was compared to the moon, and his brothers were compared to the stars — a metaphor implying that this one family was destined to rule the nations of the earth. Enmity would continue, however, between the kingdom of man (the serpent's seed which represented the world's rulers) and the Kingdom of G-d (the woman's seed which represented G-d's royal line). This theme dominates Israel's history.

The serpent was condemned to "walk" on its belly and eat dust all the days of its life. It was deemed more detestable than all the other beasts in the field. To eat dust implied the serpent would devour the earth and consume what the land produced — thereby destroying man's livelihood. The covenant promise G-d made with His people to inherit a fruitful land was never abrogated.

> I will take *Benai Yisrael* from among the nations where they have gone. I will make them one nation in the land, on the mountains of Israel, and one king will be king to them all... They will never again be defiled with their idols, their detestable things or with any of their transgressions...then they will be My people and I will be their G-d. I will cut a covenant of *Shalom* with them — it will be an everlasting covenant with them. I will set My Sanctuary among them forever.
>
> (EZEKIEL 37.21–23, 26)

In ancient Mesopotamia, the serpent, originally a neutral being, was never identified as Satan or the devil. Eventually, however, the serpent came to symbolize ancient kings who were often described as dragons (pharaoh) or beasts: like the Babylonian King Nebuchadnezzar, in the book of Daniel, who was represented by a tree and who grew so strong that G-d drove him from mankind to eat grass like oxen as he dwelled with the beasts of the field. His hair grew like eagles' feathers and his nails like birds' claws (Daniel 4.33). In the wilderness, Moses made a bronze serpent and raised it up as a banner so that those who had been bitten by snakes (kings) would look at it and live (Num. 21.8,9). Over time, the serpent became synonymous with the rulers and kings of the earth having become *the* image/idol of their gods. The *nasak* or "bite" of the serpent had to do with the financial control a king exercised over his people. By the first century, belief in angels, demons, apocalyptic battles, and the devil appeared in many Jewish texts, and Satan became the proper name for the devil (Dolansky 2017). The serpent in Revelation (12), now tied to the devil and Satan, was likely a reference to Rome's Caesar.

Pharaoh was the fleeing dragon and twisted serpent (Is. 27.1) — possibly named for his headdress, the *Uraeus* (upright form of a cobra), which was a symbol of sovereignty, royalty, and divine authority. The serpent in the garden may have also represented a powerful ANE king whom Adam and *Chavah* invited into the sacred space. For example, Hezekiah, King of Judah, welcomed messengers from the King of Babylon into the Holy Temple to show off his treasures: silver, gold, spices, precious oil, and the armory. Hezekiah's arrogance eventually opened Israel up to an attack from the King of Babylon who destroyed Jerusalem and the Temple and deported its citizens to Babylon.

Idolatry

Adam was formed in G-d's workshop and became the living image of the true G-d, not of a false pagan deity (Beale 2008: 132). In the ANE, an image/idol contained the god's presence, though the presence was not limited to the image (17). The image/idol wasn't the god but rather the god's representative as well as his slave. Adam (serving as a king-priest) was, in a manner of speaking, G-d's image/idol or image-bearer who was created to be in relationship and to reflect G-d's character, nature, and glory in the earth. To accomplish this task, G-d would eventually fill all His image-bearers with His Presence (breath) so they could serve as his living representatives in the place where He put His Name.

Idolatry is "self" usurping the role of G-d — fashioning one's own image/idol to worship. Idolatry obscures the distinction between G-d and His creation by diminishing His glory. The consequence for Israel's idolatry was exile into foreign lands where they became slaves to foreign kings and lost their unique identity. (The family of Jacob was exiled to Egypt, Israel was exiled to Assyria, and Judah was exiled first to Babylon and then in the first century to Rome).

Idolatry is a human disease that exhibits symptoms called sin. Sin is not so much a moral failure, nor falling short of one's own concept of biblical perfection, but is "man" taking the reins and deciding what is right and what is wrong. The symptoms of idolatry are manifested in a variety of ways. Addictions, for example, are generally the outward sign of the inward worship of self: substance abuse, violent behavior, pornography, gambling, sexual obsessions, eating disorders, entertainment, and on it goes. Sin continually "feeds" the idol. Addiction contaminates our temples with a foreign substance that invades the body causing its systems to shut down. Although many addictions are nearly impossible to break without outside help, our G-d is more than able to deliver those held captive. Deliverance begins, however, with denying self-rule and instead filling oneself with the Presence of G-d to overcome sin's toxic effects.

Adam shifted his loyalty from the master craftsman to himself — the image/idol the master craftsman had made.

Beale explains that by eating from the Tree of Knowledge of Good and Evil, Adam arrogated the authority to make ethical law — authority that was G-d's alone. Making ethical law was a function humans could never fulfill (135). According to Christopher Wright, Adam chose to act as if he were G-d in deciding what was good and what was evil. This is the basis of idolatry: "[When] we deify our own capabilities and make gods of ourselves and our choices." Wright goes on to say that "[a]t the root, then, of all idolatry is human rejection of the finality of G-d's moral authority" (2006: 164). Idolatry removes the responsibility of "self" to receive the Divine Presence, and the image-bearer (the image/idol) becomes a slave to the gods of this world.

Idolatry creates a breach in the created order that can only be repaired through atonement. Redemption requires payment for the slave's "release" (language of the slave market during the first century). *Yeshua* the Messiah (king) paid this price when the blood of the covenant was poured out for the "remittance" (*aphesis* in Greek; *yovel* in Hebrew) of sins. *Yovel* is also known as the Jubilee, which means slaves are released and property is returned to its original owner. The image/idol who had once been enslaved to the gods of this world has now become a new creation temple — having been returned to its original owner — *YHWH*.

Forgiveness

The sages declared that each soul within the community is a human temple. If a person is holy, then his temple is holy; if he sins, then his temple becomes contaminated. When a person repents, it is as though he rebuilds a temple within himself. Repentance (remorse, contrition) restores our humanity, and the Spirit renews our minds to think differently. True forgiveness can only happen in the place where G-d's Presence dwells. Upon returning from exile, Israel was commanded to build

G-d's house. Once the Temple and the altar were rebuilt and functional, forgiveness was available through the various offerings. It is in *Yeshua*, the new creation temple, that forgiveness is available for us.

A covenant is a legally binding contract, and, once broken, atonement is the mechanism for its repair. Atonement repairs the breach caused by idolatry and reconciles the two parties. Repentance repairs the broken bonds and should motivate the guilty party to fix the damage caused to the relationship. Forgiveness "is a personal down payment on the promise of future reconciliation. Forgiveness says, 'I just made your path to restoration possible, but only your regret, repentance, and commitment to rehabilitation can make it a reality'" (Rosenquist 2017: Vol. 2). Forgiveness is not a feeling or an emotion; it is the process for restoring the covenant and removing the chaos sin created. "If a person repents, it is regarded as if he had gone up to Jerusalem, rebuilt the Temple and the altar, and brought on it all the offerings of the Torah" (Leviticus *Rabbah* 7:2). The Torah, for its part, sets boundaries to limit the damage sin causes and outlaws behavior that reconciliation can't repair.

Once atonement has been made and repentance and forgiveness received, the consequences still remain. Acts of reconciliation help repair the damage our actions have caused. Sometimes, however, we can extend repentant apology to someone only to have it rebuffed. There are circumstances in which restitution is impossible. Sometimes the damage we both cause and suffer is irreparable. At that point, only G-d can repair what is broken. By His mercy and compassion — out of His great love — He heals the broken, binds up their wounds, and repairs the hurt. Sometimes that healing is instantaneous, other times it is not.

In due course, forgiven *priests* should leave the "hospital" of His healing mercy and return to the field to again cultivate the soil of the human heart. This happens when "the people of

God are renewed to be a royal priesthood who will take over the world not with the love of power but the power of love" (Wright 2012: 240). "Now that you have purified your souls in obedience to the truth, leading to sincere brotherly love, love one another fervently from a pure heart" (I Peter 1.22).

✡   ✡   ✡

We stand at a precipice watching what appears to be *the* most selfish, ignorant, and narcissistic culture of recent times. Solomon reminds us, of course, that there is nothing new under the sun, but the general consensus is that today's world is spinning out of control — reaping the whirlwind of chaos as this generation moves farther and farther from biblical principles. Institutions once founded upon Judeo-Christian principles, the bulwark of American society, have become compromised and corrupt: education, government, the military, media, and business. Even in the churches, there are those who refuse to stand against aberrant behavior, choosing instead to embrace the destruction of modern culture. Rabbi Daniel Lapin encourages the church to "replace timidity with nerve and diffidence with daring and determination" and to recognize there is a war against those who regard the Bible as God's revelation to humanity. He believes the very survival of western civilization is at stake (Lapin 2007: *Toward Tradition*, A Rabbi's Warning to U.S. Christians).

This nation maintains the steady pace of its death march in abandoning the most vulnerable in society: the unborn, the innocent, the disabled, and the infirmed. We live in a culture that exalts death and applauds immorality, where the media never miss an opportunity to promote this agenda — ramming it down our collective throats at every turn.

Government policies often lack wisdom and/or fail to make any logical sense. New laws typically violate biblical principles. Lawmakers, out of greed, arrogance, and/or a need to control, pass laws that pit one group against another in a fight for the same slice of the pie. Many laws have unintended consequences. Welfare policies, for example, have wreaked havoc for the family by making it financially beneficial to keep the father out of the home. The black community has been particularly hard hit in this regard. The scourge of absentee fathers (in all communities) has birthed the rise of "super-predators." Marginalized by the family and society, these sons join gangs and commit violence as they seek approval from a father figure. Some become emotionally numb, dead inside — capable of committing unspeakable acts. The traditional role of men, as protectors and defenders of the home, continues to erode to the point where young men experience utter confusion over their responsibilities and their relationships.

The problem can be traced back to the breakdown of the family which has led to the devaluing of human life. Father Jeff Bayhi (of St. John the Baptist Catholic Church), who opened a home in Baton Rouge, LA, for victims of human trafficking, laments, "We have so devalued the dignity of human life that by and large as a society we see human life as a matter of profit, pleasure or possession." He concludes that, "Human life has become a commodity. Human trafficking is one more aspect of that." A strong family is the foundation upon which a healthy, productive society is built — where the seed is loved, preserved, nourished, and protected.

That the global culture has rejected G-d is nothing new. Political, social, and religious elites of all stripes, and in every generation, are determined to eradicate G-d and His image-bearers. Their attacks have been relentless throughout the ages. They truly are beasts in the field — devouring everything they regard as a threat to their effort to corrupt G-d's image in the world.

God's will for his people in exile was that they live wisely within the pagan world where they found themselves, and because they believed God was ultimately sovereign (in ways that are normally invisible) over those nations, they were able to develop a theological account of the comings and goings of pagan nations and their rulers as well as a subversive literature and lifestyle designed to critique the pagan rulers, to encourage the faithful, and to warn of God's ultimate judgment.

(WRIGHT 2012: 172)

Escaping from the world seems a pleasant option, but the Kingdom of Heaven is not about running from trouble or finding a piece of heaven "off the grid" and waiting for the end. Jewish writings from the first century do not express this end-of-the-world mindset. The Gospel message calls His priests, who are filled with His Presence, to move into the field and mediate on behalf of mankind. Called to spread the Kingdom of Heaven over the earth, His priests contribute to the transformation of a depraved, decaying, and degenerate world. The world will never be redeemed if His covenant people abandon their mission by disappearing. "G-d's great future purpose was not to rescue people out of the world, but to rescue the world from its present state of corruption and decay" (45). The goal has always been to return to the garden, G-d's Edenic Sanctuary, to renew Adam's original vocation of making image-bearers (king-priests) of the One True G-d.

A Kingdom of Priests

Agricultural language is synonymous with created order. Before kings rose to power in the ancient world, the earth was ruled by the sun, the moon, and the stars (Gen. 1.14), which governed the cycles for planting, cultivating, and harvesting. (Joseph's dream signified a return to the original order.) For Israel, the cycles were appointed times or festivals when the people entered into the Presence of G-d to offer up the first of their harvest. For the ancient world, farming/gardening was not simply an agricultural activity. Settling the land, tilling the soil, and irrigating plants and trees were acts of creation supervised by a wise Creator. "Tending the garden" was a metaphor for upholding the created order. Priests maintained that order by growing food to sustain life for those inside the sacred space. "Bringing forth food from the earth" denoted a secure and peaceful environment, whereas the act of breaking covenant (Law) created chaos that often resulted in drought — leading to crop failure and, ultimately, starvation.

> My house lies in ruins…therefore because of you, the sky has withheld dew and the earth has withheld its yield. For I have called drought on the land, the hills and the grain, on the new wine, the oil on what the ground brings forth, on mankind and beast, as well as all labor of hands.
>
> (HAGGAI 1.10,11)

ANE scholars refer to farming/gardening as the "wisest" and most necessary of all the arts — indispensable to life. One who mastered the farmer's art was knowledgeable about the natural world. A wise farmer understood the meaning of patterns in nature: the particulars of the land, soil, wind, and rain. *Yeshua* compared the human heart to four different kinds of soil into which seed was sown: the roadway, rocky ground, among the thorns, and good soil that produced fruit. In the retelling of the Exodus at Passover, there are four types of sons (fruit produced from the seed): the wise, the wicked, the simple, and the one who does not know how to ask. The wise son eats from the Tree of Life — the Torah — in order to gain wisdom and understanding. In Deuteronomy, the Exodus is told from the farmer's point of view (26.1–5). The farmer acknowledges G-d's guidance throughout Israel's history and His role in nature.

> If you continually hearken to My *mitzvot* that I command you today, to love *Adonai*, your G-d and to serve Him, with

all your heart and with all your soul — then I will provide rain for your land in its proper season, the early and the late rains, that you may gather in your grain, your new wine and your olive oil. Beware lest your heart be seduced and you turn astray and serve gods of others and bow to them. Then the anger of *Adonai* will blaze against you. He will restrain the heaven so there will be no rain and the soil will not yield its produce. And you will swiftly be banished from the goodly land which *Adonai* is giving you.

(DEUTERONOMY 11. 13–17, ARTSCROLL SIDDUR)

Today's Kingdom priests (image-bearers) should adopt the farmer's perspective for the harvesting of souls. Although there is resistance when cultivating the human heart, the fruit, the Sons of G-d, will come forth to number the stars in the sky. The work of the priest is to replace the thorns and thistles produced by the human heart with fruit-bearing trees and shrubs (Is. 55.12,13). His Kingdom priests are to reflect His character by exercising justice, righteousness, and mercy. Wright points out that the Law is kept only if the poor, the downtrodden, and the vulnerable are cared for. Tangible love for our neighbor is the practical proof of our love for G-d. G-d sent a true king to rule with justice, making the poor and needy his constant priority (2016: 79–80). Our daily service requires that we cultivate the soil of the human heart in order to "feed" hungry souls.

The essence of the kingdom is *avodah* — service! Adam's agricultural role in Eden was a kingly and priestly function associated with service in a temple. Jastrow suggested the concept of *avodah* referred to the "space required for attending a plant" (Jastrow 1950: *Avad* entry). Service in the Temple was worship that had its expression in performing the ritual activities. "Just as the worship at the Temple altar is called *avodah*, so is prayer called *avodah*, that is service of the heart" (BT *Ta'an* 2a). The services (prayer) were the gateway for communion with G-d and instructed the worshipper in how to draw near (BT *Berachot* 24b). "So long as the Temple service is maintained, the world is a blessing to its inhabitants and the rains come down in season. But when the Temple service is not maintained, the world is not a blessing to its inhabitants and the rains do not come down in season" (the Fathers according to Rabbi Nathan 4). The priests performing the service in the sacred space transformed the world outside.

It is important to note that prayer corresponds to specific sacrifices in the Temple. "You commanded us to bring the continual offering at its set time [...] but now through our sins, the Holy Temple is destroyed, the continual offering is discontinued [...] but You said, 'Let our lips compensate for the bulls'" (*Complete Artscroll Siddur* 1985: 45). The offering being referenced, called the continual elevation or burnt offering, cemented the relationship between G-d and Israel by raising the status of the one who offered it. Every morning and evening, the priests "stood in" to splash the blood against the altar on behalf of the one who brought the sacrifice. After the Temple was destroyed, prayer became the substitute for the burnt offering. References to the continual elevation offering can be found in the New Testament: "Through *Yeshua* then, let us continually offer up to G-d a sacrifice of praise — the fruit of lips giving thanks to His name. Do not neglect doing good and sharing, for with such sacrifices G-d is well pleased" (Heb. 13.15,16). "Praying without ceasing," "praying night and day," and "continuing in prayer and supplication" allude to the continual elevation offering.

His Kingdom priests are called to finish the work Messiah began by redeeming the world from its present state of chaos. This is done by reflecting G-d's praises, as well as His justice and Wisdom, into the world through our *avodah* or service to Him. "The priesthood stands at the intersection of heaven and earth, in the Temple, in service to the Creator, with prayer, intercession, and praise on behalf of a tormented world"

(Wright 2016: 76–77). As G-d's priestly representatives, expanding His Presence to those who have rejected Him, our mandate is this: We reflect His love to the world.

What Would Jesus Do?

The question to be asked is *how* do His Kingdom priests cultivate and guard the sacred space? How do they transform the world? How do they finish what *Yeshua* began?

First, we acknowledge that we are flawed vessels, yet G-d in His mercy uses us anyway. It is His Presence that equips us to work as priests, and it is His Presence that should receive the glory for the results. We are to participate in His work as His co-heirs by multiplying His image in our sphere of influence. Even though ancient Israel failed, and often, their mandate was still to spread G-d's image — not by perfectly obeying the Torah but by exercising faith in the One who created the Torah. His image-bearers should reflect His loving rulership to the world and show those outside the covenant how they can enter into a relationship with G-d.

Priests in the Temple were responsible for preserving the sacred space: guarding, maintaining, and protecting its sanctity. In the same way, we are to guard our temple, our bodies, from becoming polluted. A process is provided for removing the contamination: repentance, forgiveness, and making restitution wherever possible. Our priestly service should begin each day with this prayer: "Create in me a clean heart, O God, and renew a steadfast spirit within me. Do not cast me from Your Presence — take not Your *Ruach HaKodesh* from me. Restore to me the joy of Your salvation and sustain me with a willing spirit. Then will I teach transgressors Your ways and sinners will return to You" (Ps. 51.12–15).

A Kingdom priest must guard against ingratitude which is often accompanied by a sense of entitlement. Entitlement, then, inevitably leads to anger and bitterness. If not dealt with, these feelings will eat at one's humanity causing apathy toward the concerns of others. Truly, ingratitude is a form of idolatry that leads to slavery. In all things, and in every circumstance, we are called to praise our G-d and model a heart of thanksgiving and gratitude to the One who created us. "A happy heart is good medicine whereas a crushed spirit dries up the bones" (Prov. 17.22).

Through prayer and intercession, priests build an intimate relationship with G-d. In turn, they instruct others how to draw near to Him. "When we are traveling toward a place of relationship, it is a gesture to diminish distance — that is the whole point of prayer. We are longing for His Presence" (*Kirvat Elokim*). Priests in the Temple were rigorously trained for service. This meant daily discipline for themselves, as well as training others through mentorship and life experiences.

BE A PRIEST who cultivates, in love, the soil of the human heart through prayer and works of service. Read and study the Scriptures every day — whole books at a time. Stay loyal and faithful to G-d's covenant. Set aside time, daily, to approach the King. Guard your sacred space, its exits and entrances, by what you say, what you hear, and what you allow your eyes to see. Protect your temple from the contamination of the culture. Don't hide in a bubble and pray to escape. *Yeshua* did not ask the Father to take those who were His out of the world, but to keep them from the evil one in the world (Jn. 17.15). Respond to every confrontation (especially on social media) with a gentle answer, for it turns away wrath. Be kind. Don't compromise your principles, ever! Act justly towards everyone. Walk in humility — esteeming others better than yourself.

As you do these things, do not be surprised when you experience hardships, misunderstandings, and/or false accusations, for the Kingdom was born out of suffering. Become involved in practical service, especially in caring for the vulnerable: widows, orphans, fatherless, disabled, downtrodden, and those without power and influence. Don't forget to pray for our persecuted brothers and sisters in the Middle East and around the world who have lost so much. Each day they face untold misery, distress, and even torture; most in the US cannot even begin to imagine what their life is like.

> Beloved, do not be surprised at the fiery trial when it comes upon you to test you, as though something strange were happening to you. But rejoice insofar as you share Christ's sufferings, that you may also rejoice and be glad when his glory is revealed. If you are insulted for the name of Christ, you are blessed, because the Spirit of glory and of God rests upon you.
>
> (1 PETER 4:12–16)

Live a lifestyle of self-discipline. Don't waste a single moment. Don't spend hours on electronic devices. The greatest time waster is social media — a black hole that swallows up even the most disciplined among us. Facebook's former vice-president lamented that social media is ripping apart the social fabric. "The short-term, dopamine-driven feedback loops we've created [including the hearts, likes, and thumbs up of various social media channels] are destroying how society works." He added, "[There's] no civil discourse, no cooperation; [only] misinformation, mistruth" (Chamath Palihapitiya in a talk to the Stanford Graduate School of Business).

Be instead a George Whitefield who once said, "What right have I, to steal and abuse my Master's time?" Largely forgotten, Whitefield (1714–1770) was *the* most famous evangelist of the eighteenth century. Called the "marvel" of his age, he delivered nearly 30,000 sermons and preached to crowds upwards of 20,000 in services that often stretched into the night. He was a brilliant orator who likely, during the course of his lifetime, preached to nearly ten million people and without any amplification. Each night before bed, Whitefield would evaluate his conduct against a list of fifteen criteria, including, "Have I been frequent in prayer? Been meek, cheerful, affable in everything I said or did?"

This daily exercise helped transform his life and mold him into one of the greatest preachers to have ever lived. The drive and zeal he possessed are incomprehensible by today's standards. So motivated was he to win souls, which he did by the thousands, that he declared, "Lord, give me souls or take my soul!" He was a Kingdom priest who utilized a not-so-secret weapon: discipline and self-control. He was motivated by a love for God that inspired him to be productive, to desire excellence, and to be willing to serve. Whitefield honored his King in all things. As G-d's image-bearer, he was a model gardener who worked tirelessly in the field, to rescue the world from slavery and death, and who waited patiently for the day when...

Adonai will be King over all the earth. In That Day, Adonai will be One and His Name One.

(ZECHARIAH 14.9)

BIBLIOGRAPHY

Alexander, T. Desmond (2008) *From Eden to the New Jerusalem*, Grand Rapids: Kregel.

Anderson, Bernhard W. (1957) *Understanding the Old Testament*, Englewood Cliffs, NJ: Prentice-Hall.

_____ (2005) *Creation versus Chaos*, Eugene, OR: WIPF & Stock.

Apocrypha and Pseudepigrapha of the Old Testament (2004), 2 vols, ed., R.H. Charles, Berkeley: Apocryphile Press.

Babylonian Talmud (1935-52), 35 vols, London: Soncino Press.

Barker, M. (2000) *The Revelation of Jesus Christ*, Edinburgh: T & T Clark.

_____ (2008) *The Gate of Heaven: The History and Symbolism of the Temple in Jerusalem*, Sheffield, England: Phoenix Press.

_____ (2011) *Temple Mysticism: An Introduction*, London: SPCK.

_____ (2014) *King of the Jews: Temple Theology in John's Gospel*, London: SPCK.

Beale, G.K. (2004) *The Temple and the Church's Mission: A Biblical Theology of the Dwelling Place of God*, Downers Grove, IL: Inter Varsity Press.

_____ (2005) *Eden, the Temple and the Church's Mission in the New Creation*, JETS 48/1 March, pp. 5-31.

_____ (2008) *We Become What We Worship: A Biblical Theology of Idolatry*, Downers Grove, IL: Inter Varsity Press.

Beale, G.K. & Mitchell, K. (2014) *God Dwells Among Us: Expanding Eden to the Ends of the Earth*, Downers Grove, IL: Inter Varsity Press.

Benner, J. A. (2005) *The Ancient Hebrew Lexicon of the Bible*, College Station, TX: Virtualbookworm.com publishing.

Bereishis (1986) 2 vols, Brooklyn: Mesorah.

Berman, J. (1995) *The Temple: Its Symbolism and Meaning Then and Now*, Eugene, OR: WIPF & Stock.

Brown, William P. (2010) *The Seven Pillars of Creation*, NY: Oxford University Press.

Buber, Martin (1947) *Tales of the Hasidim*, 2 vols., NY: Schocken Books.

Carpenter, Eugene (2009) *Deuteronomy*, (Zondervan Illustrated Bible Background Commentary), ed. John Walton, Grand Rapids: Zondervan.

Clines, David J.A. (1974) *The Tree of Knowledge and the Law of Yahweh (Psalm 19)*, Vetus Testamentum 24, pp. 8-14.

Commentary on the New Testament Use of the Old Testament (2007) eds. G.K. Beale & D.A. Carson, Grand Rapids: Baker Books.

Creation in the Old Testament (1984) ed., Bernhard W. Anderson, Eugene, OR: WIPF & Stock.

Cultural Backgrounds Study Bible (2016) Grand Rapids: Zondervan.

De Vaux, R. (1973) *Ancient Israel: Its Life and Institutions*, London: Darton, Longman & Todd.

Dolansky, Shawna (2017) *How the Serpent Became Satan: Adam, Eve, and the Serpent in the Garden of Eden*, BAS 10/13.

Dye, Dinah (2016) *The Temple Revealed in Creation: A Portrait of the Family*, Foundations in Torah.

_____ (2012) *The Fig Tree* DVD, Foundations in Torah.

_____ (2014) *Service of the Heart* DVD, Foundations in Torah.

Edersheim, A. (1994) *The Temple: Its Ministry and Services*, Peabody, MA: Hendrickson.

Exile: A Conversation with N.T. Wright (2017) ed. James M. Scott, Downers Grove, IL: IVP Academic.

Falk, H. (2002) *Jesus the Pharisee*, Eugene, OR: WIPF & Stock.

Feliu, Lluis (2003) *The God Dagan in Bronze Age Syria*, Brill Publishing.

Fretheim, Terence E. (1991) *Interpretation: Exodus*, Louisville, KT: WJK.

_____ (2005) *God and World in the Old Testament: A Relational Theology of Creation*, Nashville, TN: Abingdon Press.

Galenieks, Eriks (2005) *The Nature, Function, and Purpose of the Term She'ol in the Torah, Prophets and Writings* (PhD. Diss., Andrews University Seventh-Day Adventist Theological Seminary).

George, Arthur & George, Elena (2014) *The Mythology of Eden*, Lanham, MD: Hamilton Bks.

George Whitefield: Life, Context, and Legacy (2016) ed. Geordan Hammond, David Ceri Jones, Oxford University Press; 1 edition July 19.

Ginzberg, L. (1909-38) *Legends of the Jews*, 7 vols.

Good, Joseph (2015) *Measure the Pattern Volume 1: A Study of the Structures Surrounding the Inner Courtyard of the Temple*, Nederland, TX: Hatikva.

Hahn, Scott W. (2009) *Kinship by Covenant*, New Haven, CT: Yale University Press.

Haynes, Gregory (2009) *Tree of Life, Mythical Archetype: Revelations from the Symbols of Ancient Troy*, San Francisco: Symbolon Press.

Hareuveni, Nogah (1980) *Nature in our Biblical Heritage*, Israel: Neot Kedumim.

_____ (1984) *Tree and Shrub in Our Biblical Heritage*, Israel: Neot Kedumim.

Heaven on Earth (2004) ed. Desmond T. Alexander & Simon Gathercole, *G-d's Image, His Cosmic Temple, and the High Priest: Towards an Historical and Theological Account of the Incarnation*, Crispin H.T. Fletcher-Louis, Waynesboro, GA: Paternoster.

Hurowitz, V. (1992) *I Have Built You an Exalted House: Temple Building in the Bible in Light of the Mesopotamian and Northwest Semitic Writings*, Sheffield, England: Academic Press.

Instone-Brewer, D. (2004) *Traditions of Rabbis from the Era of the New Testament: Prayer and Agriculture*, Grand Rapids: William B. Eerdmans.

Israel, Yosef (1997) *Colorful Ceremonies in the Beis Hamikdash*, Brooklyn: Torah Umesorah Publications.

Interlinear Chumash (2008) 5 vols, Artscroll Series, Brooklyn: Mesorah.

Jastrow, Marcus (1950) *A Dictionary of the Targumim, the Talmud Babli and Yerushalmi and the Midrasnhic Literature*, NY: Pardes.

Kline, M. (1999) *Images of the Spirit*, Eugene, OR: WIPF & Stock.

Kitov, E. (1997) *The Book of Our Heritage: The Jewish Year and its Days of Significance*, 3 vols., Jerusalem: Feldheim.

Levenson, J. D. (1985) *Sinai and Zion: An Entry into the Jewish Bible*, New York: Harper & Row.

Lightfoot, J.B. (reprinted 1977) *Saint Paul's Epistles to the Colossians and to Philemon*, Grand Rapids: Zondervan.

Lundquist, John M. (2008) *The Temple of Jerusalem: Past, Present, and Future*, Westport, CT: Praeger.

_____ (2002) *Fundamentals of Temple Ideology from Eastern Traditions, Reason, Revelation, and Faith: Essays in Honor of Truman G. Madsen*, ed. Donald W. Parry, Daniel C. Peterson, and Stephen D. Ricks, Provo, UT: FARMS.

Matthews, Victor H. (2002) *A Brief History of Ancient Israel*, Louisville, KT: WJK Press.

Malina, Bruce J. (2001) *The New Testament World: Insights from Cultural Anthropology*, Louisville, KT: WJK Press.

Meyers, Carol L. (2003) *The Tabernacle, Menorah: A Synthetic Study of a Symbol from the Biblical Cult*, Piscataway, NJ: Gorgias Press.

Mishnah (reprinted 1989) trans. H. Danby, Oxford: Oxford University Press.

Mishnah Seder Mo'ed Vol. 2 (1984), trans. P. Kehati, Israel: Maor Wallach Press.

Morales, L. Michael (2015) *Who Shall Ascend the Mountain of the Lord?* Downers Grove, IL: Inter Varsity Press.

Mowinckle, Sigmund (2004) *The Psalms in Israel's Worship*, Grand Rapids: William B. Eerdmans.

Notley, R. Steven & Safrai, Ze'ev (2011) *Parables of the Sages: Jewish Wisdom from Jesus to Rav Ashi*, Jerusalem: Carta.

Rosenquist, Tyler Dawn (2015) *King Kingdom Citizen*, Ancient Bridge Publishing.

_____ (2017) *Social Media Musings* Vol. 2 Dec. 13.

Parpola, Simo (1993) *The Assyrian Tree of Life: Tracing the Origins of Jewish Monotheism and Greek Philosophy*, JNES 52 no. 3, University of Chicago.

Patai, R. (1947) *Man and Temple in Jewish Myth and Ritual*, NY: KTAV Publishing.

_____ (1979) *The Messiah Texts*, Detroit: Wayne State University Press.

Patai, R. & Graves, R. (1964) *Hebrew Myths*, NYC: Doubleday.

Pederson, Johs (1940) *Israel: Its Life and Culture*, 4 vols, London: Oxford University Press.

Petersen, Allen R. (1998) *The Royal God*, England: Sheffield.

Schachter, Lifsa (2013) *The Garden of Eden as God's First Sanctuary*, Jewish Bible Quarterly Vol. 41, No.2.

Skarsaune, Oskar (2002) *In the Shadow of the Temple*, Downers Grove, IL: IVP Academic.

Stager, Lawrence, E. (2000) *Jerusalem as Eden*, BAR May-June.

Temple in Antiquity (1984) ed., T. G. Madsen, Salt Lake City, UT: Bookcraft.

The Complete Artscroll Siddur (1985), Brooklyn: Mesorah.

The Cosmic Mountain: Eden and Its Early Interpreters in Syriac Christianity (1988). *Genesis 1-3 in the History of Exegesis: Intrigue in the Garden*, ed. Gregory Allen Robbins, 187-224. Lewiston, NY: Edwin Mellen Press.

The Old Testament Pseudipigrapha (1983-85), ed., J. H. Charlesworth, 2 vols, Garden City, NY: Doubleday.

The Works of Josephus (2000), trans. W. Whiston, Peabody, MA: Hendrickson.

The Works of Philo (1993), trans. C.D. Yonge, Peabody, MA: Hendrickson.

Thiele, Edwin R. (1983) *The Mysterious Numbers of the Hebrew Kings*, Grand Rapids: Kregel.

Tosefta (2002), 2 vols, trans. J. Neusner, Peabody, MA: Hendrickson.

Trumball, H. C. (1975) *The Blood Covenant*, Kirkwood, MO: Impact Books.

_____ (2000) *The Threshold Covenant*, Kirkwood, MO: Impact Books.

Ulansey, D. (1991) *The Heavenly Veil Torn: Mark's Cosmic Inclusion*, Journal of Biblical Literature, Spring Vol. 110, no. 1.

Vermes, Geza (1981) *Jesus the Jew*, Philadelphia: Fortress.

_____ (1997) *The Complete Dead Sea Scrolls in English*, London: Penguin.

Walton, J. H. (2006) *Ancient Near East Thought and the Old Testament*, Grand Rapids: Baker Books.

_____ (2009) *Genesis*, Grand Rapids: Zondervan.

_____ (2009) *The Lost World of Genesis One: Ancient Cosmology and the Origins Debate*, Downers Grove, IL: Inter Varsity Press.

_____ (2015) *The Lost World of Adam and Eve*, Downers Grove, IL: Inter Varsity Press.

Weinfeld, M. (1981) *Sabbath, Temple and the Enthronement of the Lord – The Problem of the Sitz im Leben of Genesis 1:1-2:3.*

Wenham J. Gordon (1985) *Sanctuary Symbolism in the Garden of Eden Story*, World Congress of Jewish Studies 9A 19-25.

White, Ryan (2017) *New Creation* DVD, Rooted in Torah.

Widengren, G. (1951) *The King and the Tree of Life in Ancient Near East Religion*, Uppsala: Lundequist.

Wright, Christopher J.H. (2006) *The Mission of God: Unlocking the Bible's Grand Narrative*, Downers Grove, IL: Inter Varsity Press.

Wright, N.T. (2012) *How God Became King*, NY: Harper Collins.

_____ (2016) *The Day the Revolution Began: Considering the Meaning of Jesus's Crucifixion*, NY: Harper Collins.

Yarden, L. (1971) *The Tree of Light: A Study of the Menorah*, London: Horovitz Publishing Co.

Yechezkel (1977), Brooklyn: Mesorah.

Zevit, Ziony (2013) *What Really Happened in the Garden of Eden*, New Haven, CT: Yale University Press.

GLOSSARY

Acharei Mot - After death, Torah portion: Leviticus 16
Acharit haYamim - end of days, the future
Adam - blood of G-d
Adamah - red, earth, ground
Adonai - Lord, substitute for YHVH
Adonai Tzv'aot — Lord of Hosts
Aharon - Aaron
Ahd - testimony
Ahzar - help
Akeidah - the binding
Akeldama - field of blood in Aramaic
Ana Beko'ach - We beg you
ANE - ancient Near East
Aravot - seventh heaven, willows, valley in the Negev
Argamon - purple
Aron - Ark
Asherah - tree, mother goddess
Ashrei - praiseworthy, honorable
Avram - Abram
Avraham - Abraham, father of many
Axis Mundi - world tree, world center
Azarah - courtyard

Ba'al - master, Canaanite god
Bakah - to split
Bamot - high places
Banah - build
Bar - grain
Barah - to create

Barah Shtei - created two
Basar - flesh, meat, gospel, good news
Bat - daughter
Bat Kol - daughter of the voice
Batsheva - daughter of seven, Bathsheba
Bat Tziyon - daughter of Zion
Bavel - Babylon, Chaldea
Beersheva - well of seven or oath, city in the Negev
Beit Avtinas - house of Avtinas, incense producers
Beit HaParvah - house of the tanning of the hides
Beit - house
Beit haMikdash - House of the sanctuary
Beit HaMoked - house of the hearth, dormitory of the priests
Beit Rosh - house is head
Ben - son
Ben Adam - son of man
Ben Elohim - son of G-d
Benai - children, plural of son
Beresheet - in the beginning, Genesis
Binah - understanding
Brachah - blessing
Brit - covenant, to cut
Brit Chadasha - renewed covenant, new covenant, New Testament
Brit Esh - Covenant of Fire
Brit Milah - covenant of cutting, circumcision
BT - Babylonian Talmud

Chavah - Eve, mother of the living
Chachmah - wisdom
Chag haMatzah - Feast of Unleavened Bread
Charan - city in northern Mesopotamia
Cheruv - cherub
Cheruvim - two angelic figures atop the Ark of the Covenant
Chilazon - snail
Chokmah - wisdom

Chol HaMoed - intermediate days for the festivals of Passover
    and Sukkot
Choshen - breastplate
Cohen - priest
Cohanim - plural for priests

Da'at - knowledge
Dam - blood
Debir - Holy of Holies
Devar - speak
Devorah - bee, community
Din - judge

Echad - one
Edut - decrees, testimony
Ehd - mist
Eish - man
Eshah - woman
Eishet Chayil - Woman of Valor, Proverbs 31
El Elyon - G-d Most High
Elisheva - my God is seven, Elizabeth
Elohim - name for God, plural of El
Eretz - earth, land
Etz - tree
Etzim - trees, bones
Etz Chaim - Tree of Life
Etz Shemen - oil tree
Erusin - second stage of marriage
Esh - fire
Even Shettiyah - foundation stone, stone of drinking
Ezrat Kohanim - Courtyard of Priests
Ezrat Nashim - Courtyard of the Women
Ezrat Israel - Courtyard of Israel

Gadol - large
Gan - garden
Gan Eden - Garden in Eden
Gat Shemen - wine press
Genizah - burial place
Gihon - belly, gush, womb, spring in Jerusalem
Goren - threshing floor
Goyim - nations

Haftarah - passage from prophets read after the Torah
HaKodesh - the Holy Place
Hakhel - gathering
Har - mountain
HaShem - The Name used as a substitute for G-d's name in
    conversation
Hekal - sanctuary
Hineni - Here I am
Hoshanna rabbah - great salvation
Hoshen - breastplate of the high priest

Ya'acov - Jacob
Y'itzchak - Isaac

Kadosh - holy, set apart, separate
Kaf - palm, shovel for the incense
Kal - complete
Kallah - bride
Kapporet - cover
Kedoshim - saints, holy ones
Kedushah - sanctified, dedicated, consecrated, set apart (can
    also be a harlot)
Ketanah - small
Kiddushin - betrothal stage of marriage
Ketonet - long-sleeved robe
Ketoret - incense

Kodesh - holy
Kodesh haKodeshim - Holy of Holies
Kohanim - plural for priests
Kohen - priests
Kohen Gadol - High Priest
Kol - voice
Korban - offering, draw near
K'por - frost

Lashon Harah - evil tongue
Levonah - frankincense
Levon - white
Livyathan - Leviathan
Luchot HaEven - Tablets of Stone

Ma'aleh Ashan - smoke rising herb
Ma'amad - standing ones
Ma'aseh Merkavah - works of the chariot
Malkat Sheva - Queen of Sheba
Malkut - kingdom
Malkut Shemayim - Kingdom of Heaven, Kingdom of G-d
Mashal - parable, proverb, dominion, rulership
Maschiach - messiah
Matzah - unleavened bread
Mayim - water
Mayim hayim - living water
Melech - king
Menorah - seven-branched lampstand
Menorot - plural for lampstand
Midrash - interpretation
Mikvah - immersion bath
Minchah - afternoon prayer service, gift, grain offering
Miriam - Mary
Mikdash - Holiness
Mikvah - immersion bath

Mishkan - Tabernacle
Mishmar - course, division
Mislei - Proverbs
Mitzvot - commandments
Mizbeach - altar
Mizrak - vessel used to carry the blood
Moshe - Moses

Nach - strike
Nasi - prince, head of the Sanhedrin
Ner Ma'ariv - light of the west, lamp on the menorah
Netzer - crown
Niddah - separate, remove from camp
Noach - Noah, brings comfort
Nun - Hebrew letter, continuing seed,

Ohel Eduth - Tent of Testimony
Ohel Moed - Tent of Meeting
Olah - elevation or raised up offering
Olam Haba - eternity, the World to Come
Olam Hazeh - This World, physical world
Omer - portion, barley
Or - light
Oren - pine tree
Orlah - forbidden, uncircumcised
Ornan - Araunah the Jebusite

Palhedrin - a chamber in the Temple
Parokhet - curtain, veil
Pargod - a curtain from the Persian language
Pelusium - Egyptian term for white garments of fine linen
Pesach - Passover

Rach - to follow a prescribed path
Rachaf - to hover, move, flutter as a bird

Rachav - proud, Rahab
Racham - mercy
Rakiah - firmament, expanse
Rav Sha'ul - Rabbi Paul
Resh - Hebrew letter, first, head
Reisheet - first, head, beginning
Rosh - head
Rosh Chodesh - new moon, head of the month
Rosh HaShanah - New Year, head of the year
Ruach - spirit
Ruach Elohim - Spirit of God
Ruach HaKodesh - Holy Spirit

Seraphim - burning
Shacharit - morning, morning prayer service
Shalach - send out
Shabbat - Sabbath, seventh, rest
Shalach - to send
Shalom - peace
Shavua - week
Shavuot - Feast of Weeks, Pentecost
Shechita - ritual slaughter
Shekan - to dwell
Shekinah - divine or indwelling presence
Shem - name
Shem HaMeforash - ineffable name
Shema - hear, Hear O Israel - opening words of the prayer
    proclaiming the unity of G-d
Shemayim - heavens
Shemot - Exodus
Sheva - seven, oath
Sheish - linen, six
Shiloach - pool of sent
Shitin - shafts
Shlomo - Solomon

Shlosha - three

Shliach - sent one, apostle

Sh'mittah - seventh year of release for the land

Shnayim - two

Shofar - ram's horn trumpet

Shtei haLechem - two breads

Shulcan - table

Siddur - Hebrew prayer book

Simcha Beit haShoevah - Rejoicing in the House of the Water Drawing

Sukkah - booth, temporary shelter

Sukkot - Feast of Tabernacles

Tahor - pure

Talmadim - disciples, students

Tamai - impure, contaminated

Tamid - daily

Tanakh - Old Testament

Targum - Aramaic paraphrase of the Hebrew Bible

Techelet - blue dye from Chilazon, a sea mollusk

Tehillim - Psalms

Tehom - the waters of the deep, the abyss

Terach - Abraham's father

Teruah - blast of the shofar

Teshuvah - repentance

Tevillah - immersion

Tikun Olam - restoring the universe

Tisha B'av - ninth day of the fifth month Av

Tishri - seventh month on Hebrew calendar, usually in Sept./Oct.

Tolat Sheni - crimson red dye from a worm

Toldot - generation, history, account, to bear children

Tov - good

Tov Ma'od - very good

Torah - instruction, law, first five books of the Bible

Tsel - shade, image

Tzaddik - righteous one

Tzitzit - fringes knotted in a special way and attached to a four-cornered garment

Tziyon - Zion

Tzemach - sprout

Ulam - porch in the temple

Yahweh - Hebrew name of G-d

Yalad - bring forth children

Yam - sea

Yamim - days

Yehoshua - Joshua

YHVH - unpronounceable name of G-d, tetragrammaton

Yireach - moon

Yom - day

Yom haKippurim - Day of Atonements

Yom Echad - One day or Day One

Yom Teruah - Day of the Blast of the Shofar

Yeshua - Jesus

Yocheved - Glory of Yah

Yovel - Jubilee, release

Zekan - elder

Zerah - seed

Zevach - sacrifice

Z'kharyah - Zechariah

Zur - scattered or estranged

The Temple Revealed in
Noah's Ark (Vol. 3)

The Temple Revealed in Noah's Ark picks up where the story of Adam and Eve left off. We move from the language of agriculture, in the garden, back to the language of architecture. Noah built a floating house/temple after the pattern of G-d's Cosmic House that we find in Genesis One. The tenth man from Adam, Noah was given the task of preserving the royal line of the kings from the destructive flood and providing a place for G-d's presence on earth. The reader will discover how Noah functioned as high priest and king and how, as king, he pushed back G-d's enemies to bring rest to the new earth. Discover answers to some of the Bible's most perplexing questions about the days of Noah in this next exciting volume of the Temple Revealed Series.

ABOUT THE AUTHOR

Dr. Dinah Dye was raised in Ottawa, Canada, in a conservative Jewish home. She attended Hebrew school, celebrated the festivals with her family, and enjoyed summers at an Orthodox Jewish summer camp. Dinah spent her teen years and early twenties deeply involved in the New Age movement. During those years, she came to the belief that truth would be based on three things: it would be easy to understand, it would be for everyone, and it would be based on love. She met that truth in 1979 in *Yeshua* (Jesus) the Messiah.

Dinah immediately recognized the importance of connecting the Gospels and the Epistles to their proper foundation in the Torah (first five books of the Bible). That understanding eventually led to the creation of her ministry Foundations in Torah. Dr. Dye holds a DMIN in Hebraic Studies in Christianity and has been uncovering Hebraic connections for nearly 40 years. Dinah's teachings are available in audio and video formats from her website. She speaks regularly at conferences and for local congregations throughout the United States and internationally.

Dinah's real passion is to help students of the Bible research and understand the Hebraic nature of the New Testament Scriptures. Much of Dr. Dye's research revolves around the Temple. She suggests the Temple is the framework for the entire Bible and holds an important key for bringing unity to a fractured community.

Dinah and her husband, Michael, live outside Albuquerque, NM and spend their free time with their grandchildren.

Foundations in Torah
www.FoundationsInTorah.com
drdianadye@gmail.com
PO Box 46182
Rio Rancho, NM 87174

Made in the USA
Lexington, KY
07 April 2018